CW00587806

ArtScroll Series®

Rabbi Nosson Scherman / Rabbi Meir Zlotowitz

General Editors

MOTHER'S

Published by

Me'sorah Publications, ltd

Musings

What we share as Jewish women and mothers

Bassi Gruen

FIRST EDITION
First Impression … May 2008

Published and Distributed by
MESORAH PUBLICATIONS, LTD.
4401 Second Avenue / Brooklyn, N.Y 11232

Distributed in Europe by
LEHMANNS
Unit E, Viking Business Park
Rolling Mill Road
Jarow, Tyne & Wear, NE32 3DP
England

Distributed in Israel by
SIFRIATI / A. GITLER — BOOKS
6 Hayarkon Street
Bnei Brak 51127

Distributed in Australia and New Zealand by
GOLDS WORLDS OF JUDAICA
3-13 William Street
Balaclava, Melbourne 3183
Victoria, Australia

Distributed in South Africa by
KOLLEL BOOKSHOP
Ivy Common
105 William Road
Norwood 2192, Johannesburg, South Africa

ARTSCROLL SERIES®
A MOTHER'S MUSINGS
© Copyright 2008, by MESORAH PUBLICATIONS, Ltd.
4401 Second Avenue / Brooklyn, N.Y. 11232 / (718) 921-9000 / www.artscroll.com

---

ALL RIGHTS RESERVED
The text, prefatory and associated textual contents and introductions
— including the typographic layout, cover artwork and ornamental graphics —
have been designed, edited and revised as to content, form and style.

No part of this book may be reproduced
IN ANY FORM, PHOTOCOPYING, OR COMPUTER RETRIEVAL SYSTEMS
— even for personal use without written permission from
the copyright holder, Mesorah Publications Ltd.
except by a reviewer who wishes to quote brief passages
in connection with a review written for inclusion in magazines or newspapers.

THE RIGHTS OF THE COPYRIGHT HOLDER WILL BE STRICTLY ENFORCED.

ISBN 10: 1-4226-0759-3 / ISBN 13: 978-1-4226-0759-6 (hard cover)
ISBN 10: 1-4226-0760-7 / ISBN 13: 978-1-4226-0760-2 (paperback)

Typography by CompuScribe at ArtScroll Studios, Ltd.

Printed in the United States of America by Noble Book Press Corp.
Bound by Sefercraft, Quality Bookbinders, Ltd., Brooklyn N.Y. 11232

To my mother

If I can give my children

but a piece of all you have given me,

they will be blessed.

Table of Contents

Kislev / Lighting the Darkness

Teves / Redefinition

Shevat / Nurturance

Adar / Joy

Tammuz / Challenge

Av / Destruction

Elul / Return

Foreword

by Rebbetzin Tzipporah Heller

I have read the beautiful insights that Bassi Gruen brings to the most natural process of all, motherhood. She sees raising a family through the *eyes* of a person of rare spiritual sensitivity. As the *Nesivos Shalom* says, it is crucial to realize that the goals that we have in raising children as Jews are radically different than the goals of parents and educators who idealize giving a child the tools to be happy, productive, and informed as a be-all-and-end-all. Giving our children means of spiritual self-expression, leading them toward having an honest and joyous connection to Hashem, and simultaneously giving them the tools to redirect or at times overcome their spiritual difficulties and limitations, is an entirely different challenge. Of course, it is a goal that can be met only by a mother who is seeking the same thing for herself. Reading this book gives an experiential handle on how this can happen.

Acknowledgments

Writing acknowledgments is proving to be one of the most difficult tasks involved in producing this book. The people I wish to thank have done so very much for me. How can I encapsulate all they are, all they have done, in a few paltry lines? But to neglect to do so would be an even greater oversight, so I shall attempt to give thanks to the many who deserve it.

This book is a collection of articles, most of which originally appeared in a bi-weekly column in the Monsey-based paper, *The Front Page*. The staff members at *The Front Page* have always been upbeat, encouraging, and a true pleasure to work with. Some of them have moved onto other jobs since I first started writing for the paper, but my gratitude to them remains. I'd like to thank Mr. Chaim Saperstein, Mr. Eli Deutsch, and all the rest of the excellent staff at *The Front Page*.

Several of the articles appeared in other publications. "First Separation" was published nearly a decade ago in *Horizons*, long before I began my writing career. *Horizons* was one of the first publications to offer budding writers a chance to be published, and I still remember the thrill of seeing my writing in print.

"Oblivious to the Music" and "Of Fares and Fairness" were first published by Aish.com, one of the leading Judaism websites. As one of their 2.6 million monthly visitors, I have often been uplifted by the inspiring pieces that they post. It is a privilege to be one of their authors, and I am grateful to Rabbi Nechemia Coopersmith for his gracious permission to use both my own pieces and some of Rebbetzin Heller's incredible material from the Aish website.

To the wonderful staff at ArtScroll: To Mr. Shmuel Blitz — for a first-time book author, he was a writer's dream. He was constantly encouraging and helpful, and ever willing to answer my *klutz kashes*. To Mrs. Judi Dick and Mrs. Michelle Katz, for their careful, yet gentle, editing. To Mrs. Miriam Zakon for her invaluable help with the subtitle, flap, and cover. To Nechama Nafisi for her delightful cover design, Raizy Knopfler for the book design and layout, and Mrs. Felice Eisner for proofreading. And to Mendy Herzberg for making it all happen.

To Rebbetzin Heller, who read this entire book and so graciously agreed to write a foreword. My gratitude goes far beyond the help she has extended on this particular project. Rebbetzin Heller has always been one of my role models; there are very few women who combine brilliance with practicality, wisdom with wit, incredible depth with incredible kindness, in the seamless way she does. Her *shiurim* have been inspiring me for well over a decade, and for her powerful inspiration, I am most grateful.

To all my rabbonim at Gateshead Seminary. It was an incredible *zechus* to spend three years in the rarefied atmosphere of Gateshead Sem. Thousands of women have found their mindsets, and their lives, transformed due to the pure, undiluted Torah hashkafah they received in Gateshead. I feel fortunate to count myself among them. Special thanks goes to Rav Todras Miller, whose ideas I used in one of the chapter introductions, and who taught us to never see life on just one level. I also wish to thank Rabbi Simcha Kohn, who influenced me far more than he ever imagined.

To Mrs. Salinger, my lifeline in the stormy waters of *chinuch*. For four years I merited to be part of her *chinuch* class. Her ideas and attitudes take me through every moment of every day that I spend with my children. My appreciation for all she has given me is profound.

To my parents. While we can never fully appreciate all our parents have done, becoming a parent oneself certainly serves as an eye-opener. It is in retrospect that I stand back and look in awe at all my parents did. Within this book are so many of the ideas and ideals they bequeathed to me. For the gift of physical life, and for the legacy of spiritual life, I thank them.

To my parents-in-law. For raising the wonderful man I married. For welcoming me into their family with warmth and caring. For being such devoted and doting grandparents to my children. For all that, and much more, I feel deep gratitude.

To my grandparents: To Me'me for sharing her wisdom, for offering endless encouragement, for enabling my dreams to come true. To Zaidy, for serving as a source of inspiration, an example of a Yid striving to be his best. To Savta Ariella, for brightening the lives of those around her.

To my uncles and aunts, some of the most fascinating people I know. It's a treat to spend time with them. I only wish it could happen more often.

To my siblings. Some families seem to drift apart once the siblings build families of their own. I'm so grateful that our family has remained close despite being spread across the globe. Each one of my siblings has added another dimension to my life.

To my dear friends, the wonderful women who enhance my life to no end. An unknown author wrote, "A friend is someone who knows the song in your heart, and can sing it back to you when you have forgotten the words." For holding onto my song, and for everything else, I thank you.

To my husband. No words in any language can express the boundless gratitude I have for the man with whom I share the awesome responsibility of raising the *neshamos* with which we've been entrusted. I am so thankful that my children have such a special person as their father.

To my children, the precious people who have made me a mother. This is a book about you, about us. Sharing my life is my choice, sharing yours is far trickier. I have tried my very best to portray our times together in a positive light, and, when things were not entirely positive, to make it clear that the blame lay with the adult involved in our interaction. I have cut lines and agonized over incidents as I tried to read this book through your adult eyes a decade hence. If, at any point in time, you are hurt by anything I have written, I am sincerely sorry. It is my hope that you will view this book as I do, as an honest account of the journey of seven people who love each other deeply.

To *Hakadosh Baruch Hu*. How absurd it seems to try to thank one's Creator. Yet how absurd it is not to. For everyone listed so far, for every thought, idea, and emotion, for every moment of my life, only comes into being because He wills it be so. The debt of gratitude is so huge it simply cannot be expressed in human terms. It is my hope and my *tefillah* that I, my home, and my life be a reflection of His will.

Ma ashiv l'Hashem, kol tagmulei hu alai.

Introduction

"Do you think I should write an introduction?"

I was in ArtScroll's Yerushalayim office signing my book contract, and I wanted to nail down all the details.

"This book definitely needs an introduction," answered Mr. Shmuel Blitz. "Make it something personal. Let people feel they are getting to know Bassi Gruen."

I had to laugh. "Trust me, Mr. Blitz, anyone who reads this book will know an awful lot about Bassi Gruen …."

Between these book covers you will find out a great deal about me, about my family, about my hopes, dreams and fears. I have had my doubts about the matter. Are my pieces too revealing? Am I sharing more than is meant to be shared?

After I had written a few "Mother's Musings," I emailed my father a sample. He wrote back telling me that he had been moved by a story. I thanked him and then wondered out loud if perhaps the piece was too personal. He answered me with a rather profound thought. He pointed out that while the outer trappings of our lives can be vastly different, inner struggles and hard-earned growth are the experiences we all share. The more personal a piece is, the more it shares one's view, the more universal it then is and the more easily it will touch others.

We may wear different styles of clothing, send our kids to different schools, and spend our vacations in vastly different locations. But every one of us has had moments of deep disappointment, of fearful uncertainty, of painful failure. Every person has experienced the bliss of connectedness, the triumph of winning an inner battle, the joy of discovering one's true strength.

This is a book about all that we share as Jewish women — as Jewish mothers. Few experiences are more universal than motherhood. We all know the thrill of the first smile, the frustration over the lost shoe, the guilt over sharp words. As frum mothers, we share an added dimension. We are familiar with the endless juggling of ideals and reality, with the struggle to grow while mundane monotony threatens to choke us. While my stories may have occurred to me alone, the emotions and thoughts beneath them will be familiar to all of you.

"The Jewish year is a mussar sefer," were the wise words of one of my seminary rabbanim. One of the antidotes to stifling monotony is to become tuned into the Jewish calendar, for it provides an endless cycle of growth, with each month offering us the opportunity to stretch another spiritual muscle.

I've divided this book according to the months of the year, alluding to the awesome potential each one contains.

This book is personal and subjective. It will show you the world through the lenses of my glasses. But it is my hope that somewhere in that vision, you will see your own reflection.

Spiritual Blueprint

Tishrei is not only a month of incredible spiritual power, it is also the blueprint of our upcoming year. Rosh Hashanah is the day on which the year is in its critical, genetic stage. On this day, we hold within our hands the DNA for all that will occur to us in the coming year. It is called the "head of the year," because just as the head controls every movement made by the body, so too, this day controls all that will unfold in the coming twelve months.

Raising children is like having a touch of Rosh Hashanah contained in every day. We receive children with pure souls — and ignorant minds. It is our job to ignite their souls, to fill their minds with the knowledge of Torah, and to focus their emotions to synchronize with Hashem's expectations of His children. We hold within our hands the raw energy that can be channeled in any direction. The words we speak today will reverberate decades later. The example we show now will be remembered when our children are parents. Rosh Hashanah, all of Tishrei, and every day of parenting as well, are times of boundless opportunity that we must use to the fullest.

First Separation

Dearest Akiva,

Your new crib arrived last week. It was the culmination of a month of shopping and selecting, debating and deliberating. I went to every large baby-furniture store in town, searching for the safest, sturdiest crib. When I finally settled on a high-quality European brand, I had to pick out a model. Then, of course, there was the dresser to deal with. Last but not least, Bubby in America picked out an adorable bumper set and the other various accessories a crib needs. Uncle Yehudah shlepped it all to Israel when he came for Succos. Two weeks later, the crib was delivered and put together.

I was so excited. I put on the new linen that I had washed the night before, and tied the bumper securely in place. Tatty hung up the diaper stacker and the fabric *Modeh Ani* that Aunt

Sora made. We arranged the top of the dresser as a changing table, and transferred your clothes from the laundry basket to the dresser. We were all set.

Then, I had an inexplicable change of heart. I suddenly felt that you were awfully little for your own room; you should stay in ours just a little bit longer. But Tatty had already dismantled the port-a-crib that had been your bed for the past five months. Now there was only one place left for you to sleep.

A few hours later you were getting sleepy. We brought a chair into your room and I fed you until your lids closed and your head rolled back on your neck. I gently laid you down in the crib and you seemed so small in such a big bed. I lingered a few more moments and then went back to my work in the kitchen. A while later, it was I who was sleepy. I went into your room to gaze at your sleeping form, to pull the quilt more tightly around you. Then I went into our bedroom which was no longer cramped ... and not quite as cozy.

But I couldn't sleep. I was missing you. I missed having the little crib wedged between our beds. I missed hearing your even breathing. I missed being able to peek at your peaceful face, to stroke the velvet cheeks. This is it, I thought, our first separation. It is the first in a long line stretching before us.

Soon I have to go back to my studies, and then we'll have to be apart for a big chunk of every day. You will be taken care of by someone who doesn't think you are the most wonderful thing that ever happened. From there, it's only a short leap to play-group, nursery, and then kindergarten. Your mornings will be spent with another woman. You'll be one of twenty-six, not the one and only. Will you let me kiss you goodbye as I leave you for the morning, or will it embarrass you?

School is next in the inevitable progression toward adulthood. No longer will Tatty and Mommy reign supreme. Rebbe will join them on the throne. He will shape you and influence you, and I will have to pray that his ideals are ones I want you to have. I will watch you make mistakes, and hopefully hold back my words, give you space to grow and explore. I will witness you being hurt by a world that can be so cruel, see the pain, and know that no band-aid or red lollypop can make it go away. Your friends' opinions may become more important than mine, their approval your yardstick. And I will have to remain firm — and yet understand.

The day will come when you, my little baby, will be bar mitzvah. I'll *kvell* and cry ... and watch you grow even further away. Bar mitzvah means high school, and I'll be grateful if you're close enough to sleep at home and if I'll get you every other Shabbos. You'll shoot up and tower above me, and pepper your conversations with Aramaic. Will you let me still kiss you, or will it embarrass you even in private?

High school is followed by *beis midrash*. No more sleeping at home. Who can waste the time that traveling requires? I'll see you every third Shabbos and send you cake and cookies. I'll look forward to Yom Tov, but you'll be busy with trips and friends and learning. I'll do your laundry and try to catch a schmooze when you come home late at night. But I'll be so far removed from your life that I can't help but wonder, will we really talk or will it be a stilted, pseudo heart-to-heart-discussion?

You will get older, and slowly your friends will begin choosing wives and settling down. Your turn will come as well. I daven already that you should find someone good, someone loving, a girl with whom you can build a home of Torah and *chessed*. Hopefully you will find her. Then there will be a *vort*, a*ufruf*, and *chassunah*. I will cry and daven and spend a good part of the dancing time glued to the mechitzah watching my little boy ....

And then you will move out of my home forever. Of course, you will come back for *Shabbosim*, for *Yamim Tovim*. With

Hashem's help, you'll bring my grandchildren with you as the years move on. But your wife and children, they will be what you call family, what you see as home. I will be the mother you try to call once a week.

And then I realized that separations are not beginning now; they began as soon as you were born. For nine months you were a part of my very being. As soon as you were born, you became a separate person. From the moment you entered this world, we have been moving apart. And that is the way it has to be.

It is three-thirty in the morning. I hear you whimpering in your crib. I rush out of bed. You turn at the sound of my voice, and look up at me pleadingly, utterly helpless, utterly dependent. I scoop you up and bring you to my bed. You happily settle down. And I? I stroke your blond fuzz, kiss your tiny forehead, and hold you very close.

With more love than you can imagine,
Mommy

Rosh Hashanah
at the Sandbox

"**I**t is during the day of Rosh Hashanah that G-d and His Heavenly Court sit in judgment on every individual. The heavenly ledgers are opened and every person's deeds are counted and scrutinized."

"Mommmmmmy, he's throwing sand in my hair. Tell him to stop." My head jerks up from the ArtScroll machzor and I blink in the bright sun.

"Don't throw sand," I say rather ineffectually. "Here's a bucket; put sand into this." I wait a moment more to see that my instructions are not being entirely ignored, and then return to the page I was reading.

"The Talmud speaks of 'the ledgers of the living and the ledgers of the dead.' Since the subject is the judgment of Rosh Hashanah, it is clear that even those referred to as dead, are still alive. What then, does the Talmud mean when it refers to the 'living and the dead'?"

At the sound of a high-pitched shriek, I look up. My toddler is hanging from the top of the slide, having tried to jump down the side. I leap up, race to the slide, and gently place her on the ground. A quick hug, a drink from the bottle of juice we brought along, and peace is restored.

I go on reading, absorbing the concept that from a spiritual standpoint, we are alive only if our lives have meaning and spiritual depth. Otherwise, though we may breathe and eat and work, we are spiritually dead. "The Day of Judgment now begins," the *machzor* exhorts. "No one is condemned to remain in the category of the wicked or vacillating, because this is not only the Day of Judgment, but the first of the Ten Days of Repentance. Let this be the theme of the day's prayers, thoughts, and deeds."

"Mommy, push me on the swing; come push me." My four-year-old is calling me. I struggle to get to my feet — expecting a child makes my every move cumbersome — and walk over to the swings. I push again and again, while my daughter sings "Dip the apple in the honey" at the top of her lungs.

Suddenly, the serene morning air is pierced by a great blast. The shofar is being blown in the shul across the street. Again and again, the shofar trumpets, wails, calls. I try to focus on the sounds, try to absorb their message.

"I'm hungry, Mommy," the request breaks my reverie. "Where are the pretzels?" I walk over to the bag I packed and rummage around until I find the pretzels. This initiates a spate of "I also want ...," which is followed with cups of juice for all.

Somewhere, I think, people are hearing this shofar inside a shul. They are standing there with nothing on their minds other than their relationship with their Creator. They are concentrating on Hashem's kingship, His greatness, and His glory, and there is nary a pretzel to be seen. As I pour juice, they are standing to begin the *tefillah* of Mussaf, their only task to focus upon the lofty words they are uttering. They will actually daven from the machzor, not just scan the Overview.

I try to fight the feelings of unfairness, the sense of being cheated out of the essence of this holy day. I try to remind myself that the same G-d to Whom I wish to be praying is the One Who gave me the circumstances which placed me in the park right now. I try to focus on the enormous blessing of having children to keep me tied down.

Wishing to maximize my opportunities as a mother, I gather the children around me and talk about the greatness of the day. I try painting a picture of mighty scales standing before Hashem, making sure to stress the mitzvos of not fighting and *kibud av v'em*. I tell them a Rosh Hashanah story. It's inspiring while it lasts, but soon enough, they are back at the monkey bars, climbing, bickering, laughing, spending the day much as they spend any other day in their young lives. A part of me keeps yearning for something loftier than sand and snacks.

The kids are getting fidgety. "Hey, guys," I call, "let's go home. We'll have popsicles and play Memory." This is greeted with enthusiastic responses, and soon I'm surrounded by the three of them clamoring to hold my hand. Lacking three hands, I have them settle on fingers.

Back in the house, I settle them down with their icy treat, slide a kugel into the oven to warm up, and begin shuffling Memory cards. As my children chatter, I find myself mentally reviewing the past year and the events that occurred, all of which were decided on the past Rosh Hashanah. So many blessings, so many tragedies. As I face the unknown of the coming year, there is so much for which I dream.

I need life. As I focus upon this most basic of needs, I can sense my unborn child.

I want a true connection to my Maker, to serve Him with my heart, not just with my actions.

"I want to hold your hand, Mommy."

I require protection from myself, from my negative impulses and non-productive thoughts.

"Mommy, I'm falling, come get me."

There are the more mundane, but essential parts of life for which I need help — livelihood being high on the list.

"I'm hungry, Mommy."

My desires, hopes, and requests are echoes of those I've been hearing all morning. A hundred times a day, I'm in a position to fulfill the needs that mirror my own. How am I responding? Am I giving my children the type of responses I hope to receive? Do I give them the attention, love, and kindness that I yearn for from my Creator?

People stand in shul crowning Hashem as King. Here, in my living room, I can do the same, by mimicking in the faintest of fashions His endless giving.

"Mommy, let's play already." My children are eyeing the Memory cards I've laid out.

"Sure. Come sit in a circle." And for the first time all day, I am focused entirely on them.

A Whole
Broken Heart

Considering what was at stake, I was appalled at my apathy.

It was the second night of Rosh Hashanah, the day when all of mankind is judged, their fate for the coming year decided. My head knew the significance of the day. It insisted that I spend the day in the most spiritual of pursuits to set the tone for a year of growth. I arranged for a babysitting switch with a friend, so both of us would have the opportunity to daven in the holy atmosphere of a shul, away from dolls and peanut butter. My head led me to read explanations of the *tefillos* and essays about the meaning of the day.

It was my heart that seemed to have gotten stuck in another realm. It remained untouched, full of the petty concerns and worries that occupy it for the majority of the year. My head did all the right things, but I felt as though a metal barrier existed between my head and heart, the action of one unable to move the other. I was frozen, unable to stir myself to try to reach out for a deeper relationship with the King Who was so near.

I was grateful when my younger sister offered to watch my children so I could daven Ma'ariv in shul. Perhaps the uplifting tunes and the power of dozens of people turning to their Creator in unison would move me. I walked the short distance and slid into a seat just as the chazzan began intoning the ancient melody, signaling the beginning of the *tefillah*. I started to daven.

After several minutes, having finished before the chazzan moved on, I took a quick look around me. With many women at home preparing the festive meal for their family and guests, the women's section was rather empty. I spotted her easily.

She was around eight years old, her glossy brown hair held back by a beautiful ribbon that matched her floral dress. In her hands was a shiny new siddur. What struck me was the way in which she was praying. Small head bent over the pages, lips articulating each word carefully, she was entirely engrossed in communicating with her Maker. Nothing distracted her, not the door opening behind her, not the lady coughing beside her. Utterly sincere, she seemed to appreciate the importance of what she was doing, and prayed with a single-minded intensity.

Noticing her oddly-shaped eyes and unusual features, I realized this young girl was a Down Syndrome child. Suddenly, my locked heart opened with a painful jerk. Looking at this perfect soul in an imperfect body, I couldn't help but compare it to my own situation, a perfect body perhaps, but housing such an imperfect soul. I became excruciatingly aware of my limitations and faults as I stood before G-d next to this innocent child. I began the work of the day, taking a brutally honest look at where I was in relationship to G-d, reflecting upon His greatness, and thinking of where I truly wanted to be.

Down below, the davening continued and I followed along. But it was an eight-year-old little girl who was leading the *tefillah* for me. I kept stealing glances at her. She never noticed. She sat davening, slowly, carefully uttering each word — an act that was clearly an effort for her. Her face reflected serenity in doing what she knew was right. I ached, I longed, I turned to G-d and begged Him to help me reach that place — to help me serve Him with simplicity, with honesty, with sincerity. I begged Him to help my heart become as whole as hers.

Eventually, davening ended. The young girl kissed her siddur and walked out the door. After several moments I walked out as well, in a very different state than when I had entered. The metal barrier had dissolved; the frozen emotions had thawed. The Kotzker rebbe used to say, "There is nothing more whole than a broken heart."

A shining soul clothed in a limited body had helped me reach that state.

Cats Don't Fight on Yom Kippur

*J*ust a few hours remained before Yom Kippur would draw to a close. The children and I had spent the day playing Candy Land, visiting the park, and reading books. Hoping to obtain a few minutes of inspiration, I was setting out for shul with my three younger children in tow. They each clutched bags bursting with nosh and were eying them greedily.

"Not now," I kept warning. "You can eat those only once we reach the shul's porch."

There were two paths leading to the street we needed. One involved a straightforward flight of stairs, the other, a set of ramps.

Since I was pushing a stroller, I opted for the ramps. As I headed toward that path, I waited for three-year-old Devorah to relinquish her cherished spot holding onto the side of the stroller and scamper down the steps. There are overgrown shrubs on both sides of the ramps, and they are a favorite hiding spot for cats. One day, two warring cats, hissing and scratching, had leapt out of the bushes as we made our way down the path. That experience was enough to keep Devorah off the path for good. I was puzzled, therefore, to see her march happily beside me.

"You're going down the path?" I asked with a show of nonchalance.

"Of course," she replied blithely. "Cats don't fight on Yom Kippur."

Cats don't fight on Yom Kippur. The surety, the conviction, with which she stated the fact, struck me. There was no doubt in her mind that on the holiest day of the year, it was simply inconceivable that any creature, even the scruffy stray cats, could engage in bad behavior.

Could the same be said about us? Could G-d look down from above, gaze at His nation, and state, "People don't fight on Yom Kippur"? I certainly hoped so. Wrapped in a tallis, feeling both dizzy and euphoric from the lack of food, and spending virtually the entire day engaged in prayer, certainly helps put one in a state in which fighting is far from tempting.

But the purpose of the day is not simply to spend the day as angels and then come crashing back to earth as coarse humans. It is to hold on to a tiny bit of the angel within and incorporate it into our lives. Perhaps that can be helped by listening to the simple statements our children make — statements that often contain fundamental truths.

"I didn't show Dovi my candy because he didn't have one, and if he'd see it he'd feel bad." I pat the child on his head for sensitivity. But do I think along those lines when I relate my kids' latest antics to a woman struggling with infertility? When I purchase an object beyond the means of most of my neighbors?

"The teacher only likes the kids who are smart." The statement may horrify me, but am I willing to befriend someone I feel is not sharp?

"I'll only share my birthday bag with you if you let me play with your ball." I sigh, and try to teach my child about altruism. But don't the conversations around my kitchen table, while compiling a guest list for a simchah, sound rather similar?

Unencumbered by years of absorbing social niceties, and unfamiliar with the shadowy half-truths that inhabit the world of adults, there's a brutal honesty to that which children say. It pays to listen and hear the messages they send us through their prattle.

Kids see the world in black and white; grey doesn't show up on their inner radar. While that's not always positive, when it comes to evaluating our own behavior, when it comes to the introspection needed at this time of year, it can be a very helpful perspective to incorporate.

The Clouds

ivka rolled the perfect white orbs between her fingers. Sixteen years of eating the heavenly bread hadn't dulled her wonder. She didn't toil over fires, spending endless hours preparing food; it was Hashem's love that they ate meal after meal, day after day. The one duty which remained, she did with care. She set the table, and placed the manna in the beautiful dish she had "borrowed" from her Egyptian mistress before they had left the country forever.

As she waited for her husband and sons to return from their daily learning session, she glanced outside. The sun was beating mercilessly on the sand dunes that stretched endlessly as far as the eye could see; but the air around her was pleasant. The Clouds of Glory ensured that the nation of Hashem would never be uncomfortably hot. She looked up, and there they were above her. If she strained her eyes, she could see more of them on the edges of the encampment: the fluffy, white masses surrounding them on all sides.

These clouds did far more than just keep the people cool. They protected them, deflecting the arrows of the enemies surrounding the incipient nation. They flattened any mountains and filled all valleys that lay in the path of the Jewish people, ensuring that their trek through the desert would be as effortless as possible. Why, the clouds even washed and ironed the people's clothes. The backbreaking labor of scrubbing clothing by the riverbank was but a distant memory. Her Creator's love — it was everywhere she looked.

--------·•·•·--------

Three thousand years and six thousand miles away, her descendant, Raizy, is working feverishly in her kitchen. She's taken the day off from work, and wants to maximize it. She skillfully spoons a meat-and-rice mixture into cabbage leaves, deftly tucks in the corners, and carefully places them in the sauce simmering on the stove. This was the recipe her Bubby Rivka had always made; the one she had received from *her* bubby. Raizy wonders how many generations of women in her family have made the same stuffed cabbage. In the oven, two trays of flaky potato knishes are reaching crisp perfection, and on another flame, the borscht is bubbling. As she places the last cabbage roll into the pot, Raizy stops for a second to inhale the fragrances around her. It smells like Succos.

The peace is shattered when her children burst through the front door, the kindergartener arriving at the same time as her big boys. The kitchen table is quickly covered with a half-dozen hand-made succah decorations. Despite their lopsided appearance and runny colors, Raizy always finds them so much more beautiful than the tinsel ones her children entreat her to buy each year. Her *yeshivah bachurim* fill the house with their laughter and their laundry, and black hats litter the living room like exotic houseplants. She spots the rectangular *esrog* boxes piling up on top of her breakfront. The salads in her fridge are sharing space with *haddasim* and *arovos*, wrapped in damp paper towels and silver foil to keep fresh. Raizy rushes around, trying to cram a week's worth of work into this one stolen day.

Seven hours later, Raizy is bringing the steaming platter of stuffed cabbage out to the succah. She serves dish after dish, and finally sinks gratefully into her seat. She takes a moment to look around. At the head of the long table sits her husband — her confidant, her provider of both spiritual and physical sustenance, her best friend. Next to him sit two lonely men he often brings home from shul.

Looking at them, she's suddenly keenly aware of her loving extended family, her comfortable home, and the dozens of blessings that are so deeply a part of the fabric of her life. The rest of the table is crowded with her brood, dressed in their new Yom Tov finery. Her oldest is fingering the wisps beginning to appear on his chin. The baby is turning her bowl of stuffed cabbage onto her freshly washed hair, and the others seem to be eating, talking, and singing all at once. Her eyes linger briefly on each child.

Raizy looks up. Between the reeds covering the succah she can see the luminescent moon and a sprinkling of stars. Great masses of dark clouds flit by. And for an instant, they seem to be the Clouds of Glory themselves.

Her Creator's love — it's everywhere she looks.

Ever So Much More So

"Look, Mommy, come look!" There is breathless rapture in the high-pitched voices entreating me to come see their handiwork. I allow the little hands to slip into mine and pull me out of the kitchen, past the living room, and into the succah.

It is transformed. Just two hours earlier there had been only the bare wooden walls. Now those walls are adorned with pictures of Torah luminaries and my offspring's attempts at art. Glittering foil chains zigzag through the succah, and plastic fruits peep out from between the s'chach.

"Mommy, isn't it beauuutiful?" Menucha croons. Her eyes, big with wonder and delight, look up at me expectantly.

"Yes, sweetie, it certainly is," I reply. I take another look, and suddenly, instead of seeing simply another succah with its typical array of shiny decorations, I catch sight of it from her perspective. I am able to see a wonderland, a palace, a seven-day dream that we all helped create. The succah is larger, roomier, more spectacular, when I see it from her eyes.

"It's stunning," I say again, "and you helped make it so special." She beams.

Two days later, my husband walks in from davening on the first day of Succos, bearing aloft his *lulav*, cradling his magnificent *esrog*. There is an air of regality about him. The children leap up from the tower of blocks they are assembling and crowd around, each eager for the opportunity to hold the *arbah minim*. My husband hands them to me first. We all walk out to the succah. Four pairs of eyes are upon me as I carefully unwrap the *esrog* from its protective flaxen wrapping and position the *lulav*. Akiva is shaking with impatience for his chance to say the berachos. The girls are enraptured by my every move. Even the baby tugs at my skirt. My spectators help me focus on the unique opportunity literally in my very hands. I close my eyes, and the *Shehechiyanu* I recite is said with fervor.

———◆———

As a young girl, I loved reading about the escapades of Homer Price, an enterprising and mischievous young fellow living in Anytown, USA. His comical antics and unusual encounters keep the small town rocking. In one story, a slick stranger comes to town and offers a magical powder for sale. The invisible "ever-so-much-more-so" powder will enhance whatever it is sprinkled on. Put a dash in your coffee, and it will be ever-so-much-more aromatic. A bit on your silk blouse and it will be ever-so-much-more smooth and silky. A helping on your French fries and they will be ever-so-much crispier.

While I can't remember the end of that story, the wonder of the idea remains. Imagine a powder that would be able to make all the good things in life that much better, the comforts more comfortable, the treats more enjoyable. It's an intriguing and tantalizing concept.

It came as a surprise to realize that I have that powder — four containers of it, to be exact — within my home. For life with these little people is an endless stream of "ever-so-much-more-so" experiences.

As an adult who has lived through scores of *Yamim Tovim*, it isn't always simple to experience the appropriate enthusiasm and excitement for each one. But when a seven-year-old come home bursting with the new ideas he learned about the Yom Tov, I am awakened to what is approaching.

Spending much of Yom Tov in the kitchen, it is all too easy for me to forget to look past the pots and see the importance of the day. The meaning of Pesach gets coated with scouring powder; the essence of Succos hidden under the menus and meat order. Shiurim help, and sometimes that shiur can come from a five-year-old. "Mommy, do you know that each of the *arba minim* is like a different Jew, and we hold them all together just like we're supposed to be together?!" If I just absorb the messages they themselves can't truly understand, my Yom Tov may look very different.

"Ever-so-much-more-so," a succah can look ever-so-much-more beautiful when our children decorate it alongside us; a Shavuos night-learning session can seem ever-so-much-more lofty when accompanied by a young son; a Pesach Seder can be ever-so-much-more uplifting when we share it with our offspring. All we have to do is open the container.

CHESHVAN / חשון

Concretizing Good

Cheshvan can be a disconcerting month. After a Tishrei of high-charged spirituality, of visiting realms reserved for angels, we suddenly find ourselves back in the monotonous routines that comprise the majority of our lives. The contrast can be jarring.

We can connect the two months and bring the power of Tishrei into Cheshvan by fulfilling the promises we made and by carrying out the resolutions we undertook during the lofty yamim noraim. True spirituality does not reside exclusively in shul during Neilah; it shows its face at the dentist's office and at PTA meetings, through burnt suppers and missing socks. A connection to Hashem depends not upon having the right atmosphere, but the right attitude. During our lives we live through years of Tishrei, often followed by decades of Cheshvan. Those lucky enough to attend seminary usually experience a year brimming with inspiration, overflowing with ruchniyus.

Then marriage comes and the blessing of children. Suddenly mornings means mitzvah notes and forgotten lunches rather than a Chumash shiur and a hashkafah class. Afternoons are defined not by Minchah and study sessions, but by supper preparations and the baby's physical-therapy session.

Holding onto the long-ago inspiration is tricky at best. But it is also the true test of how well we understand the nature of spirituality. When we can infuse our Cheshvans with the same glow we experienced in Tishrei, we have come a very long way indeed.

The Aftermath

*I*t's all over. The majesty of Rosh Hashanah, the awe of Yom Kippur, the joy of Succos, and the exuberance of Simchas Torah. Now I'm faced with laundry piled sky-high, a fridge full of unwanted leftovers, and an unending exhaustion. A friend calls. I tell her that I think the bears have a good thing going when they hibernate for the winter.

———•◦•———

Chol Hamoed. We make a pilgrimage to the Kosel. I had managed to daven there a few months earlier, but the kids had not been at our holiest place for a full year. I'm wary about bringing four young children there. Will they appreciate its significance? Even more basic — will they be able to stay silent long enough so that those around us could appreciate its significance? I decide to come well-armed. I buy a roll of citrus-flavored hard candies for each child. Hopefully the treat will allow me, and everyone else, to daven a decent Minchah.

We reach the ancient wall, turning golden in the rays of the setting sun. After passing endless throngs of people, I manage to find two white plastic chairs. I sit my two girls down and hand them the rolls of candy. "First, daven to Hashem for whatever you want," I instruct. "Then, you can have these candies. Eat them one at a time, and suck them — don't bite." I open my siddur, and hope for the best.

Two minutes later, I hear my nearly-seven-year-old Menucha talking to four-year-old Devorah. Menucha, my dainty, feminine girl who spends endless time in front of the mirror trying new hairstyles, who doesn't particularly like school, who loves jumping rope, sleeping late, and collecting napkins, is speaking about *tefillah*.

"You're already eating your candies?" she asks Devorah. "You finished davening? But there is sooooo much to daven for." I steal a glance at the pair. Menucha's eyes are big, and her face earnest. "I davened that Hashem should make my eyesight better [she'd just recently been diagnosed with a lazy eye, and started wearing glasses and a patch]. I davened that we should all be good, that the poor people should have money, and that the sick ones should get all better. I asked that Shlomo and Chana should have a baby, and that Mordechai and Rivky should both find a shidduch."

Devorah looks at her in silence, absorbing all her requests. "All right," she finally says, "I'll daven that I should be a talmid chacham."

"Devorah," Menucha sounds exasperated, "you can't be a talmid chacham. You're not a boy. You have to daven that your husband should be a talmid chacham. I asked Hashem to send me a big, big talmid chacham as a husband."

"Okay," says Devorah, ever agreeable. And she resumes sucking her sweets.

A few minutes pass. Then Menucha begins talking again.

"You see all these people, Devorah?" Her voice is laced with the wonder of it all. "Some of them aren't even frum. And they all want to be here. You know why? We used to have a Beis Ha-Mikdash, and then bad people destroyed it. They burned it all down — everything but this wall. It's all we have left of the Beis HaMikdash. So it's very kadosh. That's why everyone wants to be here."

"Oh," says Devorah in a voice that sounds suitably impressed. And the sucking continues.

As I look up at the wall, which is growing darker as the night envelops us, and see the white doves circling, cooing above, I feel an intense gratitude for that rare feeling that perhaps I'm doing something right.

———•◦•———

It's Simchas Torah night. We've traveled to Yerushalayim for Yom Tov so my husband can spend the day in his yeshivah. After prolonged singing, the first hakafah begins. In this yeshivah, the Sifrei Torah are piled high on the bimah, and the men and boys dance around, rather than with, them. In the very center dances the Rosh Yeshivah. His face glowing with joy, radiating holiness, he dances before the scrolls that define every moment of his life. Around him, in circle after circle, are his exuberant students. My eye picks out my husband. Then I search for my eight-year-old son. It's the first time we've allowed him to attend these late-night hakafos, and I hope that he'll be dancing and not playing tag outside. I spot him. In the very middle, just a few feet from the Rosh Yeshivah, dance a small group of young boys. Feet pounding, eyes glowing, they sing and sing, their trebles rising above the rich baritones of the men. And my child, he's right there among them. Dancing before the Torah, legs leaping and spirit soaring high. And my soul soars as well.

I fold the laundry with tired movements, as the roast is re-heated for the third time. The kids bicker in the background. It's all over.

But need it be all gone?

All-Knowing?

"**J**ust one, Mommy, please." They look up at me expectantly, big eyes pleading. They've had too much sugar already, but I begin to waver.

"We were so good when you took a nap." The clincher. I hand them each a taffy and they scamper off in delight. For the moment, at least, I'm the benevolent, wonderful mommy bestowing my largesse upon one and all. But I'm not fooled. I know that in an hour or two, I'll have to say "no" to some request, and then I'll be transformed into the wicked witch of the west, a tight-fisted, mean mommy.

Ah, the power of mothers. "Can Shani sleep over tonight?" "Can I make candy apples for Shabbos?" "Can you buy me that new watch all the other boys are wearing?" "Can I have another piece of cake?" The stream of requests is endless, and we are supposed to have the wisdom, knowledge, and experience to know when to give and when to withhold, when to tap into our love for them, and when to focus on their need for disciplined lives. As long as our children have not yet hit their teens, we remain these mighty human beings who hold the keys to fulfilling the majority of their wishes and dreams. And our struggle is to use those keys well.

Sometimes, though, the task seems too daunting.

Every so often, one of my children will request something, and I find myself looking down at the little person in bewilderment. *Why are you asking me?* I wonder. *I haven't the foggiest idea whether fulfilling that request will be beneficial or detrimental to your chinuch. Why don't you find some mature, knowledgeable adult and ask* **her**? Reality, and those expectant eyes, pull me back, and I'm forced to formulate a proper response. The child drifts off, elated or aggrieved, and I'm left with a sense of amazement at the number of decisions expected of me in the course of a day, a week, a lifetime.

I'll never forget the first time I realized my mother was human like the rest of us, and that the answers she gave with such surety were not the result of a direct pipeline to heaven.

My paternal grandmother would visit us one weekend every three months. Those two-and-a-half days would be a delightful time of being loved and spoiled. Among the many treats she would shower upon us was a jumbo box of high-quality Barton's chocolates. I haven't seen the confection in nearly two decades, but I can still picture the box. Each chocolate was individually wrapped in colored foil, and there was a myriad of shapes. The shapes were not just decorative — each harbored a different filling. The fun lay in discovering what each one was. Would you bite into a crunchy nut, a rich truffle, or a semi-liquid raspberry cream? The only way to find out was to try one. Each Shabbos, every child was allowed to choose one chocolate from the box. We loved it.

One Sunday afternoon after my grandmother had gone home, I was bumbling around the house, trying to amuse myself. Then I spotted the box of chocolates stowed out of reach on top of the freezer. Out of sheer boredom, I asked my mother, who was folding laundry nearby, if I could have a chocolate. In my wildest dreams I didn't imagine the answer would be affirmative. My mother looked at me for a moment, and then — she said YES!! The world stopped spinning for a moment as I tried to absorb my shock.

"Why'd you say *yes*?" I blurted out before I could think better of it.

"Because I was tired of saying *no*," my mother replied.

Tired of saying *no*?! My seven-year-old brain struggled to absorb the significance of this statement. Does this mean that sometimes it's hard for her to say no? Could it be that sometimes the responsibility of wisely parenting a big brood is heavy upon her shoulders? Could my all-knowing mother, who has an answer for *every* question on earth, be a mere mortal, with doubts, insecurities, and worries, just like the rest of us? The chocolate was gone in no time, but I had enough food for thought to keep me busy for weeks.

The time will come when our children suddenly see us beyond the role of "mother." That day they will realize that we have our own battles, tests, and dreams. The moment they comprehend that many of our decisions regarding their upbringing are, at best, a shot in the dark as we struggle to raise them into happy, productive adults. And that moment will change our relationship forever.

There's another moment that needs to be reached, and the sooner it's reached, the better. We have to view our offspring beyond the role of "our children." It is easy to mistake the tiny baby we bear for a body we must feed, bathe, and clothe. He grows a bit, and becomes a soul we must develop and mold. And all that is true. But if that's the sum total of our relationship, it will be a shallow relationship indeed.

Our job is to step outside our role as parent and take a good look at our children from the outside. What kind of friends, students, and siblings are they? What makes them tick? What are their pet peeves? Their greatest hopes? Their biggest fears? How do these people view the world, their school, their family, their mother? Are our expectations of them a reflection of their capabilities or of our unfulfilled dreams?

We all know it is important to truly get to know our children. But in the rush of life, our goals sometimes become feeding all the little mouths, as opposed to hearing what they have to say; getting them all into bed, as opposed to discovering what they think about once they are there.

When we take the time to listen and learn, there's a side benefit. The better we know our children, the better equipped we'll be next time they ask, "Mommy can I ...?"

Longing

*C*haviva Wolf rifled through the morning mail. The electric bill (she tucked that one in back of the pile), a bar mitzvah invitation, a reminder from the head of the shul's dinner committee, a ten-percent-discount ad from Murphy's tires (that she tossed), and then, a handwritten letter.

She blinked when she saw the return address. Her Miri? A letter? It was hard for her to imagine Miri writing anything that didn't require a keyboard and a screen. Miri, of the bouncing auburn curls, of dance troupe and cartwheels, the girl who ran rather than walked — any form of communication that required that she wait more than a few moments for a response made her uncomfortable. But here it was.

Chaviva sat down and slit the envelope eagerly. She pulled out the two sheets of paper filled with Miri's easygoing scrawl.

And there was a sharp stab of longing for the little girl who had left her and traveled across the globe.

Dear Tatty and Mommy,

Probably surprised to get a letter from me — no? Bet you didn't realize I even knew where to buy a stamp. Well, it's one of the many things I'm figuring out this year. There were things I had to tell you which the pen could say more faithfully than the tongue.

Chaviva grinned. Only those close to Miri knew that beneath the bubbles and bounce was a girl with deep thoughts, and the power to express them in an eloquent way.

I'm writing this letter to thank you. I know I'm a bit early; I'm supposed to put all this mush into the letter I give you at the end of the year with whatever gift I bring home. But that will be what everyone does. I want to really thank you and to do so right now.

I LOVE it here. The country, the city, the school. I love the blazing blue of the sky; the gold of the stones in the setting sun; the black of the frocks, jackets, and *bekeshes*; the white of the scarves and aprons the women wear here Friday night. I love the teachers and the taxi drivers, the rabbis and the beggars, the whole cacophony of my nation living in their Land, at the feet of their King.

And as if all that isn't enough, there are the classes. Seminary is a whole new world. Sometimes I feel like my brain will split open All those questions that buzz around on the edge of your mind while growing up; the questions you're too scared to confront — they answer them here. *Fundamental* is the word that keeps coming to mind. You learn how to live, why to live, what to live for.

The Torah has become something alive, breathing and palpitating with meaning and significance. The words, the ideas, they all fit, like some elaborate tapestry that I've only come to see just now. I wake up each morning and there's nowhere on this entire planet I'd rather be, nothing I'd rather be doing. It's the most exhilarating of feelings. And for all that, for giving me this chance, I thank you.

Chaviva sat still for several long moments, staring at the sheets of paper. Then she stood up, stretched, and went to tackle the overflowing sink. Tuesday was the day she went into work late. She had a few golden hours all her own during which she was meant to create some sort of order from the chaos that surrounded her.

As she scrubbed a stubborn bit of last night's lasagna from a Pyrex dish, Chaviva marveled at how twenty years before, her own emotions had been so similar to those her daughter was now expressing. She remembered walking the narrow streets, trying to gulp in the holiness, as though she could store it some place deep within and draw on it in later years. She remembered sitting mesmerized in class, listening to her teachers and marveling at how oblivious she had been to the beauty of her heritage. And the longing that laced everything she did. The longing for the Land, for the lifestyle she was being exposed to, for the world she was discovering.

At nineteen, Chaviva had her life mapped out before her. At twenty-nine the cracks were beginning to appear. By thirty-nine, she looked at the map and couldn't recognize half of the landmarks.

The only thing that remained was the longing. It kept itself well contained most of the time, tied neatly away with the rest of her unfulfilled dreams and unspoken desires. But every once in a while it broke through the barriers and came bursting forth, until her entire being became one huge ache for something more, something different, something holier and more sublime.

The longing came now, all in a rush. She wanted her daughter's wonder, her purity, her belief. She wanted a world that was defined by *midrashim* rather than mortgages, *pesukim* rather than pasta. But it was more. She wanted to want. Her tears mixed with the dishwater.

Chaviva finished the dishes and wiped down the counters. She headed to the basement to tackle the mountain of laundry. But as she passed the kitchen table, she couldn't resist. She sat down and began rereading the letter. And suddenly she realized that there was another page she hadn't noticed earlier.

Thanking you for sending me is only one part of the picture. There's something far more fundamental (told you that word is *everywhere* these days) for which I owe you gratitude. And that's for helping me become the type of the person who could utilize this opportunity. Some of the girls here see this year as one long party. And I can't fault them. I have no idea how they grew up.

I watched you, Tatty, learn for hours each day, both before work and in the evening, no matter what, no matter how. And I saw how crazy you'd make yourself, Mommy, to make sure that he never, *ever* missed those sessions.

I watched you both listen to Torah tapes and fill the house with appropriate books. I saw how you always had a Shabbos table with Torah talk and how you spoke to a rav whenever life threw you something you couldn't handle. I watched you bite your lips when you wanted to say something you shouldn't, and try to keep from screaming *even* when you were hopping mad, and never did I see the two of you fight.

I watched people who lived their lives not as though they *had* to listen to the Torah, but as though they *wanted* to. And that made all the difference in the world.

With all my love,
Miri

And for the first time in two decades, the longing seeped out of Chaviva, not because it was replaced by despair, but because it was crowded out by joy.

Life's a Bowl of Strawberries

*Y*esterday was one of those days. My seven-year-old, Menucha, came home and exuberantly informed me that we had been chosen for the honor of baking one of the two cakes which would be served at her siyum. She also mentioned that the date of the siyum had been changed — it would be taking place tomorrow. Until she walked in, I had been feeling quite accomplished. I had put up supper in the crock pot that morning — a rare achievement for me — and made a nice, hot lunch. I was done with cooking for the day — or so I had thought. Now, we had a new reason to get the kitchen dirty. After my initial sinking of heart, a new realization dawned.

Just for the record, I'm quite a decent baker, honest. Desserts were the first things I learned to make when I ventured into the kitchen at the age of 12, and I was soon my family's dessert chef. Over the years, I've built up my repertoire and expertise, and I can make many a tasty treat. There's one caveat though; my desserts are created for mouths, not eyes. I've never had the patience to master complicated creams and fancy chocolate swirls. I have no inclination to make cream puffs in the shape of swans or checkerboard cakes. I admire those who do; I enjoy their food at simchas. But we all have to know our limitations, and these are mine.

That being the case, how do I compete at a class siyum when the other mothers seem to wield the icing tubes like old pros? A while back, I had hit upon the solution — I'd make a strawberry shortcake decorated with kiwi and strawberries, and let the beauty of G-d's handiwork adorn my cake. I prayed fervently that we wouldn't be chosen for cake duty before strawberries came into season. Here in Israel, we enjoy them fresh for but a few months, from Chanukah until Pesach. I breathed a sigh of relief when we weren't chosen to make the cake for the siyum on *Bereishis* or *Noach*. By *Lech Lecha*, strawberries were just appearing in the supermarket at outrageous prices, and by *Vayeira*, they were everywhere you looked. Now, the second grade was having a siyum on *Chayei Sarah*, and finding strawberries should be a simple task — providing it's any day of the week other than Sunday.

Stores are utterly emptied of produce before Shabbos, and remain in that state until the fresh delivery arrives on Monday. Nobody buys fruits or vegetables in Israel on Sunday. It's just one of those things. So now, I was stuck. The cake had to be baked on Sunday, but how would I obtain the strawberries that would be my ticket to a fancy cake?

Seeing my distress, my husband valiantly offered to brave the howling winds and pouring rain and walk to the biggest supermarket in the city, ten minutes from our home. I gratefully agreed, and sank into bed for a nap.

When I woke up, my husband was gone and a bag of frozen strawberries was defrosting on the counter. My daughter informed me that the store had not had any fresh strawberries, so my husband had opted for the frozen ones. There was one minor problem. The frozen variety sported a hechsher other than the one approved by the school as the only one allowed at class events. We were in desperate need of "plan B."

I called my neighbor down the block who makes fancy cakes and knows all there is to know about anything with sugar. She told me the small grocery on the corner had had a slew of strawberries on Thursday, and may still have some in stock. If I'd wait until five, when the store reopens for the afternoon, I could call and check. She mentioned that I could make the cake with canned peaches sliced thinly. She told me that if I was really desperate, she thought she still had some frozen strawberries with the right hechsher that she had squirreled away the year before.

Feeling calmer, I rounded up the kids and made a double recipe of the shortcake. I carefully poured the batter into two huge round pans, and slid them into the oven. A niggling voice told me that the cake on the higher rack might rise too high and hit the ceiling of my small European oven, but in desperation, I ignored that voice. Then my daughters and I settled down to play card games.

We were in middle of our third game when the smell of burning began to fill the house. I raced to the kitchen and yanked open the oven door. The entire top of my delicate cake was stuck to the top of the oven, burnt to a crisp. I took a knife and hacked the cake off the oven ceiling. Then I pulled out the rack. As I pulled, chunks of cake fell away. In my hands was a cratered mess just half the size of the cake I had placed in the oven shortly before. My daughter's crestfallen face mimicked mine. After a brief moment of despair, I rallied. "We'll cut off the burnt part and cover it all with cream, and it will be just fine," I said in as authoritative a voice as I could muster.

Now, the hunt was on for strawberries. The corner grocery was finally open, so I called and asked if they had any *tutim* (strawberries in Hebrew). When the clerk asked me what type I wanted, I was puzzled, but told them regular ones were fine. A minute's pause, and she told me that yes, they had them in stock. When I asked if they were still in good condition, she sounded baffled and said yes. So Menucha went out in the rain to the grocery — and came back empty-handed. Utterly frustrated at this point, I called again. "Sorry, geveret, I thought you asked for *p'titim* [orzo], not *tutim*."

Time for "plan C." I rummaged in my large pantry for the big can of peaches I always keep there. It was nowhere to be found. Then I remembered the trifle I had made a month earlier with canned peaches. I had never restocked. What was "plan D"?

My younger ones were clamoring for supper. As I dished out supper, I called my neighbor again. She checked her freezer and yes, she had the strawberries. We were on. Poor Menucha trudged out again, and returned with two small bags of icy strawberries. I let them defrost as I finished with dinner and raced the kids through bath time. Finally, we were ready for assembly.

I whipped up a big carton of whipped cream and we began. First we buried the mutilated cake in cream. Then we spread the defrosted strawberries on top. More cream for the top, and then the remaining strawberries and a cut kiwi allowed Menucha to create a beautiful design for the top of the cake. It looked lovely. It tasted good, too. I had used the extra batter to make a little loaf pan for us and I was very pleased with the results. Breathing an enormous sigh of relief, I slid the cake tray into the fridge and turned to face a filthy kitchen.

The next day, Menucha carried the large cake to school with pride and joy. As I closed the door behind her, I thought about how no one would know the amount of effort that had gone into that cake. Then I eagerly awaited her triumphant return from school. I couldn't wait to hear how our cake had been received.

Menucha seemed subdued when she walked in. "How was the cake?" I prompted. "Did the girls like it?"

A pause. "They threw it in the garbage. Not all of them. Some of them ate it, but a lot of them threw it out. They said it looked nice ...." Her voice trailed off and she went to wash for lunch. I sat rooted to my place, too disappointed to respond. What had gone wrong? I'd probably never know.

Five minutes later, I had to leave the kitchen table abruptly to interview a pediatrician for an article I was working on. I tried to banish shortcakes and strawberries from my mind and focus on his replies to my questions.

Several minutes into our conversation, the doctor mentioned that the ultimate goal of a pediatrician is to make himself expendable. "It's amazing what medicine has accomplished in the last decades," he said. "A hundred years ago, only half the children born lived to adulthood. In fact, many claim that in the Middle Ages, people didn't bond with their children until they were at least five years old. They were too afraid of developing a deep connection to a child they would very possibly lose."

I let this morbid bit of information sink in. One hundred years ago, people considered it perfectly normal to lose half the children they bore. Of course, they themselves didn't have too long of a life to look forward to — the average life expectancy was a mere forty-five years.

The interview continued, but in the back of my brain this information kept buzzing. I thought back to last winter. My then-one-year-old had gotten a bad case of pneumonia. His fever had topped 104 and he had lain glassy-eyed and utterly apathetic in my hands. I was genuinely scared. At the doctor's office, a quick x-ray confirmed the initial diagnosis of pneumonia, and the doctor prescribed strong antibiotics. We gave him the medicine, and to our utter astonishment, within two hours he was racing around once more, his high-pitched laugh filling the house.

On the phone with a friend later that night I had mentioned how blessed we were to have antibiotics. "What would have happened to Shlomi if we didn't have such medications?" I had wondered aloud.

"He probably would have died," my friend bluntly responded.

Now all this ran through my mind. And suddenly, the saga of my rejected cake shrank to its rightful proportions. Looked at from this perspective, my life was a jumbo bowl of cherries — or was it strawberries?

A Kiss
From Above

I'll never forget the day I was almost run over by a bus. I was in Yerushalayim, trying to squeeze too many errands into too little time. Rushing to get to some store before it closed, I reached a small side street off a major intersection. I looked both ways, and stepped into the street.

Then I heard the roar of engines. A bus had suddenly pulled around a bend in the street and was rocketing toward me. For a moment I froze. I was in the middle of the street, and this red-and-white monster was bearing down on me, tons of metal that could crush me in a moment. Should I run to the other side? Race back to where I stepped off the curb? I was paralyzed with fear. Then my brain leapt into action. I quickly backed up to the curb behind me. The bus whizzed by, inches from my body, and I slumped against a nearby wall.

Several people around me were just as shaken as I. One elderly woman just kept looking me and shaking her head in relief. Another roundly denounced the profound irresponsibility of the bus driver. One man turned to me and said, "You should *bentch gomel*," before he disappeared in the crowd. I took a few deep breaths, and then crossed the street and walked to the store.

But the images kept intruding. What if I hadn't gotten to the curb on time? Would I have survived? Would I have been crippled for life? How would they have told my husband? My parents? What of my children — I may never have seen them grown up; they may have had to face the remainder of their lives motherless. Each thought was more horrific than the preceding one.

For the next week or so, I felt an overwhelming gratitude toward Hashem. I had been given the greatest gift of all — life — and I wanted to use it properly. I had been spared. There was a palpable sense of closeness to my Creator. He had plucked me from danger and left me unscathed.

———•◦•———

Two days ago, for no particular reason, I found myself reminiscing about my two favorite frum novels as a child. There hadn't been all that much available back then, and there were only two books that I truly loved. I'd read each one numerous times, and felt intimately connected to the characters.

As I thought about those books, I reflected on how much I'd love to be able to share my childhood favorites with my own children. How I'd love to see them enjoy the same books I had loved. But I realized that there was a good chance that they were no longer in print, and had disappeared from the bookstores.

I made a mental note to begin searching for them as soon as I could. And then my mind moved on to other matters.

The next night I was up late cooking for Yom Tov. At midnight my cell phone rang. It was my husband. He had gone to buy a lulav and esrog, and had been successful in his search. Now he was about to head home. But he had noticed that a neighbor of the esrog seller was having a book sale. There were dozens of books piled on a table outside their apartment.

"I spotted that book you've mentioned so many times," he said, naming the title of one of my favorites. "And I remembered how you loved it. Should I get it?"

"Sure," I responded jubilantly. "And maybe she has the other one, too?"

"Yeah, right," my husband responded with a laugh. He then patiently went through the piles, reading titles to me. Suddenly there was a pause.

"Bassi," he said excitedly, "you won't believe it, but I just found your second favorite book."

"Grab it," I told him, as though he was fighting mobs of shoppers at the tiny sale at this unearthly hour. He did.

A short while later, he came home bearing the loot. I was thrilled. And very grateful. What were the chances that 24 hours after I had thought of two old favorites my husband would stumble across both of them in the hallway of the apartment building of his esrog merchant? Hashem's Hand was oh, so evident. Like the woman whose husband brings home a bouquet of her most prized flowers, or a box of her favorite chocolates, I felt cherished and loved. I had received a kiss from above.

———•·◦·•———

There was a story that one of my rabbanim in seminary was fond of relating. One of the gedolim in pre-war Europe — I've forgotten who — didn't want his daughters attending the State-run schools. So he decided to homeschool them. One of the state requirements was that the students write a short essay daily. So this gadol instructed his daughters to write down one personal incident of *hashgachah pratis* every single day. Doing so, he explained, would sensitize them to the many small and large ways Hashem personally cares for them. Our seminary teacher suggested we do the same, and many of us took up the challenge.

At first, it was very difficult. Life in seminary was wonderfully monotonous — great shiurim every day, day after day. Study sessions. Breakfast, lunch, and supper. A jaunt to the laundromat or the pharmacy. Nothing too earth-shattering. When and where were all these incidents of *hashgachah* supposed to happen? But once I started looking, I started seeing.

"I really needed to speak with Dini, but was having a hard time finding her, and then there she was across the table when I sat down for lunch."

"We had a speaker who said just what I needed to hear. And then I had a chance to put his words into action that same day."

"We were on a hike and I wasn't feeling well. Just then the bus, which was meant to pick us up farther along, drove by and let a few girls on. I was one of them."

The fact that I knew that I'd have to write something in my little book that night kept me alert and attuned to the myriad manifestations of my Creator's love. During the two years or so that I kept this going, I felt perpetually connected to my Father in Heaven.

There are times when Hashem shows us His *hashgachah* in full force; when life hangs in balance and we are saved by Divine intervention. But to wait only for those moments to feel our Father's love is to lose out on the day-to-day outpouring of care. Not always will His messages come as a dramatic shake; sometimes there is a just a gentle tap on the shoulder, a subtle whisper. It is up to us to attune ourselves to hear it.

Perhaps no time is as suitable for such work as immediately following the grandeur of Tishrei. After a month of high-voltage spirituality, after being swept through four *yamim tovim*, one on the heels of the next, it's often hard to return to mundane routine. Life seems flat, and we wonder how the intense feeling of connection can dissipate so fast. Looking for the little instances of *hashgachah* that light up every day can nurture and sustain that connection over time.

It can be the appointment you should have missed — save for the fact that the doctor was running late. It can be the chance comment that reminded you of the birthday you'd have otherwise forgotten. It may be finding a parking space in a crowded lot. Instead of saying "How lucky" and moving on, pause for just a moment and allow yourself to feel the kiss from Above.

KISLEV / כסלו

Lighting
the Darkness

Kislev falls out during the short, cold days of the winter. Chanukah, the most pivotal event of Kislev, is about the few vanquishing the many, the pure defeating the defiled. We celebrate Chanukah with tiny flames — tiny pinpricks of light that can dispel great darkness.

There are a number of central concepts in Yiddeshkeit that are compared to light — Torah, mitzvos, neshamos. There are many ways we can light up the vast darkness that threatens to engulf us, many candles we can grasp when we fear we have lost our way.

A mother must not only be a candle, she must also be a match. Shedding light for those around us is but the first step. Our mission is to help our children find their own illumination, to ignite the unique light that is hidden within each soul. We do that when we focus upon the light within them, even when their behavior is fueled by the darkness in this world. If we never lose sight of their light, if we consistently reflect it back to them, it will eventually light up not only their lives, but the lives of all those they reach.

The Light Will Prevail

Yerushlayim 3623 (138 BCE)

*D*ina took her hands from her face and stepped back from the candles she had just lit. The tiny flames danced in their pottery cups on the table. Beside the door, in the niche specially carved for the occasion, the flames of the menorah vied with the Shabbos candles for attention. The whole house was bathed in light.

How different life had been just a short while before. Then she had lit candles while huddled in a dank cave. Her family's Shabbos meals would be conducted in hoarse whispers while the threat of annihilation by the ruthless Greek soldiers hung over them like a stifling black cloud. They'd just managed to escape with their lives when they circumcised their youngest son. Her neighbors had not been so lucky. Now she was raising their children as well as her own.

She had almost succumbed after that. The constant terror had seemed too weighty a burden to bear. Her siblings, her cousins, and most of her friends had given in long ago. They were leading carefree lives: attending the theater, soaking up the foreign literature, reveling in the culture of the Greeks. How they mocked her — clinging to an ancient, antiquated religion. It was Shlomo, her husband, who served as a bastion during those dark days.

"Hashem and His Torah are all we truly have, Dina," he told her again and again. "You'll see. One day the light will prevail."

Then a tiny band of fearless Kohanim had arisen to fight the mighty Greek army. The Hellenists had laughed; the loyal Jews quaked in fear. Surely this impossible mission would end in failure and embitter their lives even more. They had steeled themselves for the inevitable.

It had never come. Victory followed victory — and one glorious day the Beis HaMikdash was theirs once again. Shlomo's face had been infused with a glow she'd never seen as he took his flute and hurried off to the holiest spot on earth. He would once again join the other Leviim in singing praises to his Creator.

He returned haggard. The desecration and destruction he had witnessed had been almost too much to bear. But a smile played upon his lips as he recounted the painstaking search of the Kohanim to find oil that had not been defiled. They had unearthed one tiny flask of pure oil, and tonight the Menorah would glow once again.

The next day he returned in a state of astonishment. The oil was still burning. She and the children had hurried to witness the miracle for themselves. Crowds were gathered outside the Beis

HaMikdash, all focused on the flickering flames. Her relatives suddenly shed their Greek tunics and couldn't face her when they met her in the street. For eight days the miracle had continued. The light of those tiny flames seemed to fill the entire earth.

Exactly one year had passed. The Chachamim had instituted a new holiday. Every year, for all generations, they were to light their menorahs, sing Hallel, and give praise to Hashem. Her sacrifices, her inner battles to remain strong — they would affect not only her life. They would touch the lives of all her descendants. These eight days would be infused with spiritual power until the end of time. The light had prevailed.

Madrid 5297 (1537)

Miriam bolted the door, pulled the curtains over the windows, and turned to face her husband.

"The Montagues were caught last night when they lit their menorah."

Yosef was silent. No matter how careful they were, no matter how many precautions they took, the church always seemed to be one step ahead. Sometimes it was the maid who noticed salted meat. Sometimes it was a neighbor who spotted flickering flames on Friday night. Sometimes it was the greengrocer who reported suspicious vegetable purchases in April. The possibilities were endless — the end, the same.

"They're to be burned in the next auto-de-fé. Let's stop. I can't live this way. Is my life not worth more than a few candles?"

"A life without our heritage, with no connection to our G-d, is not worth living," her husband replied firmly. "If you're willing to give up all this ..." and his hands swept in an expansive gesture to take in the palatial residence, the sumptuous gardens, the jewels upon her neck, "we can try to flee to Holland. They say it's good there for the Jews."

She felt crushed between two terrible realities, torn between the chances of losing her life or losing life as she knew it. That night, sitting in the cellar of her mansion, she stared at the menorah's flames for a long time.

Two weeks later they were on a boat headed for Holland.

Chicago 5763 (2002)

"You're coming, Carol, aren't you?" Tony asked the question lightly, but the words hung heavily in the air. Most girls would have jumped at the chance to attend the Romano's annual holiday party. It was a lavish affair attended by the city's upper crust, and talked about for months. But ever since she had had her first holiday invitation at the age of five, Carol's mother had ingrained within her that Jewish girls don't belong at those parties.

And Carol knew that Tony didn't want to bring her simply as a friend. He wanted them to debut as a couple engaged to be married. Just the day before, he had shown her the holiday present he had bought for her — a dazzling four-carat diamond ring. He had spoken of the golden future they would share. He had reminded her of how deeply they cared for each other. Did it really matter that the party would include unfamiliar carols and a towering, tinsel-wrapped tree in the corner of the room? Should she give up a chance for happiness simply because Tony had not been born a Jew?

Tony was waiting for an answer. "We'll talk later," she demurred. "I have to be getting home."

As soon as she entered the house, she sensed something different in the air. There was an electricity, a hushed anticipation. Then she saw it. The simple brass menorah, the one her great-grandfather had brought with him from Kiev, lay waiting upon the windowsill. An hour later it was glowing brightly, and the smell of potato pancakes filled the house.

The storm in Carol's soul raged all night. But as the rising sun tinted the sky a pearly pink, she was infused with an inner calm. She had an answer for Tony. That ring belonged to another girl. She had a different destiny.

To Make
Mommy Proud

O n the first day of Chanukah, my daughter's school had a *chanukas habayis* for their new building. Considering that the school had spent a decade moving between cramped apartments and poorly-insulated caravans, this was a big celebration.

Living in a relatively new settlement, I have become so accustomed to finding shuls, schools, and even the municipality housed in caravans that a real brick-and-mortar building was exciting for me as well. The first day of school, all the mothers accompanied their daughters to admire the graceful semi-circular structure, the sun-drenched classrooms, and the enormous yard.

Now this was a real school. But the electricians were still finishing the wiring, and the contractor was putting final touches on the paint, so the gala event celebrating the new building was pushed off until Chanukah.

How the school prepared! A professional choir leader, Toby, was brought in from Yerushalayim three times a week to head a choir comprised of all the students from first through eighth grades. The kindergartens prepared their own presentation. Activities were planned, and speakers arranged.

Finally, the great day arrived. Clutching a container of parsley dip (it was the parents who provided the refreshments), I set out with my daughters. Due to a lack of additional funds, the school contains just classrooms and offices, without the added amenity of an auditorium. But for intrepid Israelis this proved no problem. The weather had been unseasonably warm, and the yard was large enough to accommodate everyone who would come. The girls were to perform on the stairs, and the mothers would sit in plastic chairs facing them. Tables off to the side were groaning under an outpouring of homemade refreshments.

The one detail the school hadn't taken into account was the fact that during the morning hours, the school building blocked the winter sun from reaching the yard. Combined with brisk winds, this resulted in a very cold venue. The principal got up to give the introductory address. Repeatedly pulling her coat tighter around herself, she was clearly as cold as the rest of us. Then the microphone malfunctioned. So she spoke at the top of her lungs.

"I love Israel," whispered my good friend, seated to my left. I looked over so I would catch the rolling of the eyes that I was sure accompanied the statement. It wasn't there. My friend was smiling. "The people are so unpretentious, so natural," she explained. Sounded like a good attitude. I tried to focus on all the fresh air I was getting.

Eventually, the mike kicked in, the principal finished speaking, and the show was on. First the little ones marched in, proudly waving flags sporting the school's emblem. Problems arose when the first little girl inexplicably stopped in the center of the top stair, causing a domino-like congestion. But she was quickly nudged into place and the girls were soon standing in rows before us, beaming and waving their flags. My eyes searched for my treasure. There she was, in the center of the middle row, face creased in serious concentration as she tried to perform each motion perfectly. I waved, and she favored me with a tiny grin.

In no time, the first song was done, and the kindergarten students were being ushered off the stage. Next, the oldest four classes came on and sang a beautiful rendition of "Baruch haba." Halfway through, the younger four classes marched in, took their places between the older girls, and sang along. I was impressed with the costumes, struck by how the school had once again managed to create an eye-catching effect with few materials. Each girl was dressed in the ubiquitous white shirt and blue skirt mandatory for any sort of celebration. But on top of that, they had satin collars and cuffs in shades of red, orange, and yellow. As they moved their hands, the cuffs produced a shimmering rainbow of color.

I spotted my older daughter on the far left in the second row. She was beaming — at me, at the other mothers, at the whole world. My Menucha loves performances of any kind; they bring out the very best in her. She sang heartily, eyes glowing, ponytail bouncing, hands waving in graceful motions.

Toby, who was also the choreographer, stood in front of the girls. Her hands moved in sweeping gestures, and she walked back and forth as she tried to ensure that all two hundred girls sang and moved in time to the music. She had clearly done an excellent job teaching them. Each clap, each sweep, each flick of every hand was in perfect synchrony. "Baruch haba" was followed by the words of the *birkas habayis*, the blessing for every home, put to lilting music. Next there was a Chanukah song.

Suddenly, as the music was already beginning for the next song, the principal rose and picked up the microphone. "Toby's mother just got here from Yerushalayim," she announced. "She was stuck in traffic. Now, in her honor, we are going to sing 'Baruch haba' once again." A smattering of applause. Then two hundred girls all began singing the song they had sung just ten minutes before, so Toby's mother could hear it. So she could have the nachas of seeing the wonderful job her daughter had done.

I took a good look at Toby. She was in her mid-thirties. She probably has a number of children of her own. Yet, just as my daughter kept seeking me out in the crowd to make sure I was watching, to ascertain that I was enjoying the fruits of her labor, Toby had the same dream. And the principal was sensitive to the dream of every daughter — to have her mother see her accomplishment, to share her moment in the sun.

It seems no matter how old we are, or how far we've come in careers and life, as long as our mothers still walk upon this earth, we want their approval, their support, their nachas. "Look Mommy," we say in the subtlest of ways, "aren't you proud?" And their beaming smiles reward us like nothing else can.

Bubby: The Light Extinguished Last Chanukah

I was in the toy store when I found out she was no longer with us.

It was the first day of Chanukah. We were planning to visit my husband's grandmother in the evening. It's hard for her to get out and shop, but she wanted to give my children presents. I promised I'd pick out gifts. Running for the bus, I realized that I had uncharacteristically forgotten my cell phone. Never mind, I consoled myself, I wouldn't be gone for more than an hour or two. What could be that urgent anyway?

I spent a magical hour in the toy store. The child within was having a fabulous time, taking in the dolls and the trucks, the board games and the balls. Should I get my kids arts-n-crafts? Play food? A train set? Should I get one jumbo gift or something for each of them? I finally settled on three games, and then moved over to the aisle of games for my unmarried siblings. A tricky card game caught my eye. Did they have it already? I reached for my cell phone — only to realize anew that it was on my kitchen table back home. Undeterred, I asked the store proprietor if I could use her phone; this was business for her after all. She readily agreed, and I dialed my mother. My sister answered.

"Hi," I chirped. "Is Ima home?"

A silence. Then, "No, she's with the *chevrah kadisha*."

My stomach fell. Fighting waves of panic, I asked, "She's where?"

Another silence. "You don't know?"

"Know what?" I was screaming now, dizzy with fear.

"Bubby. She was *nifteres* this morning. The *levayah* is in a few hours."

And here I was in a toy store, clutching a stack of games. Somehow I paid and got out of the store. As I raced back home, it wasn't the boisterous school children or the harried shoppers that I was seeing.

I was picturing my Bubby's home in Baltimore. I could see the plastic covering the hallway carpet, the plastic that made such a satisfying, scratching noise if you rubbed your shoes on it. There was the green couch in the living room from which shoes were banned, and the bronzed leaves my uncle had brought from California. There were the carpeted steps we loved bumping down, and on the shelves, the Russian *matryoshka* dolls we never tired of opening. The kitchen had blue plastic swivel chairs that turned around and around until you were utterly dizzy, and an old-fashioned bread box we peeked into nearly every time we passed it.

Best of all, Bubby's house had Bubby. Usually in the kitchen cooking something delicious, surrounded by wonderful smells. "Don't walk in the kitchen," she'd entreat, "the cake will fall." So we'd tiptoe around waiting for the cake to emerge, high and golden. No matter how many times I got her blueberry crumb-cake recipe, mine always turned purple from the pie filling, while hers came out in three perfect layers.

Friday night was the best of times. After the meal, Bubby would serve tea and cake. She'd put out everything — the sugar and lemon, the cookies and cake. Then she'd serve everyone tea, and finally bring a glass for herself; she could only drink tea if it was straight off the flame. My Zaidy used to tease her, saying she had an asbestos tongue. After we'd enjoyed our tea party, we'd move to the green velvet couch, with a pile of old photo albums. Few things gave Bubby more pleasure than look-ing at pictures of her children and grandchildren and kvelling. I was fascinated to see my mother as a girl, but I marveled that Bubby's wonder was as great as mine, despite her having seen each picture countless times.

As our family grew, she found it harder to host us all, and started visiting us instead. Each time she came, the back seat of the car would be loaded with trays of meatballs, kugels, and cakes. She brought the greatest gifts, too. For a grandmother, she was amaz-ingly aware of the coolest things to buy for a teen-aged girl. She bought me a hand-painted pink shirt with a funky belt, which was the envy of my friends. She remembered the colors of my uniform and had a hair clip made to order. When I commented five times on the cake-decorating set I found on her basement shelves, she gave it to me as a gift before I went home. Her gifts were a giving of self, a clear sign of how important we were to her.

My Bubby was always young at heart. When I was twelve, I spent two weeks alone with her and my Zaidy. Late Motza'ei Shabbos, when the last dish was washed, wiped, and put away ("If you leave the dishes in the drainboard, they'll have water spots"), she said, "Let's go for a drive." This was a novel concept to me — to get in the car and drive nowhere? But that's exactly what we did. She and my grandfather sang and sang and pointed out various landmarks — the school my mother had attended, the house that used to be their shul. We ended the night at a twenty-four-hour store, buying a treat for us all. I'll never forget that drive.

Now, as I neared my home, other images of my Bubby came to the forefront. This was a different Bubby; a Bubby suffering from advanced dementia, handicapped and in pain. It was a Bubby who didn't know me, who would thrill at the sight of my children, but not realize they were her very own descendants. For ten long years, Bubby — our laughing, energetic, hard-working Bubby — slowly slipped from our grasp, claimed by an illness that stole her very essence.

I thought of my most recent visit, the visit that had suddenly become "the last time I saw her." She was in the hospital, in a comatose state. She was bloated and looked so different from the woman I loved. I had come with my tiny six-week-old son. While her devoted Filipino caregiver watched the baby outside, I spoke to Bubby. I told her about the new great-grandson she had. I described the bris and informed her that it had been her husband — my Zaidy — who had been the baby's sandek. I held her hand and rubbed her shoulder.

Did my soul sense it would be our last time together? I found myself telling her how much I loved her. Could she hear me? I didn't know, but I wanted her to be aware of the sunshine she had brought to my life. I reminisced about the custom-made hair clip and her luscious coffee cake. I reminded her of the stories she would tell us and how she always had time for our tales, no matter how long they may have been. Pausing frequently to wipe away the tears, I told her how much she had meant to one little girl, and how much a grown woman missed her smile and love.

Now Bubby has left us. She will suffer no more. How does one mourn when all has already been lost? By the time she was taken, only her shell had remained. Our Bubby we had mourned long before. And yet, she had still been with us. Now Bubby is truly gone.

This Chanukah will be her first yahrtzeit. My brother and his wife were blessed with a baby girl last week. They called her Shifra, after my Bubby. A little bit of Bubby is back with us. But the real Bubby — oh, how I miss her.

Scissors, Markers, and Glue

After eighteen months of waiting, my four-year-old's hair was finally all one length. I felt like celebrating.

I'm not partial to bangs — at least not as far as kids are involved. Bangs fall in eyes and food. They get in the way of pictures, and thirty-six hours after the last haircut, they already manage to have that shaggy, overgrown look that is usually associated with an Old English Sheepdog. All these reasons have brought about my policy of, "Until you are old enough to care for your hair yourself, it stays one length."

However, reaching that blissful state of "all hairs synchronized in growth" can take a while. I was therefore thrilled when, during a routine trim, I noticed that Devorah had just hit this milestone.

It lasted all of fifteen hours.

Looking at her over spaghetti and meatballs the evening after her haircut, something kept niggling at my consciousness, but with the noise and demands that characterize supper hour, I couldn't figure out what was disturbing me. Only as I got her into pajamas did the awful truth dawn on me.

She had bangs.

Not just any bangs. These bangs were entirely uneven: starting off almost non-existent on one side of her forehead — a few fluffs of hair — to ridiculously long on the other side, that awful length that is too short to fit behind the ears and too long to stay out of eyes.

"What happened to your hair?" I screeched. She looked at me uncomprehendingly for a moment.

"Here," I gestured, ruffling the offending bangs, "what happened?"

"Oh. Menucha cut them," she informed me, "just like you cut my hair last night."

I was so worked up I could scarcely talk. I gave her a lecture. I gave Menucha a lecture. I gave Menucha a punishment. And then I told them again how upset I was. Every time I glanced at Devorah, I had to refrain from getting angry at Menucha again.

Two weeks later, I walked into my home office to discover some changes in the décor of the room. My trusty yellow highlighter had been used to add a fluorescent touch to the walls, the sofa bed, and even the metal window frame. Only after a moment's thought did I realize that my toddler's recent growth spurt now allowed him to reach my desk — and my writing implements.

I tried unsuccessfully to scrub the marks away. The wall could always be repainted, although that was easier said than done.

But the sofa bed will never be the same. Since there is little use in lecturing a seventeen-month-old, the only one I could be irritated at was me. And irritated I was, every time my gaze fell on the garish yellow streaks on the black print of the sofa bed.

Only much later, when I calmed down sufficiently to view both incidents objectively, was I able to realize how natural it is to cut your younger sibling's hair and to scribble on walls and furniture. Who among my acquaintances has not had a similar experience, either in the role of mother or as the impromptu barber or artist? These occurrences are so commonplace they have become passé. They won't even elicit sympathy from the park-bench mothers or laughs from grandmothers. These mishaps are simply part of family life.

This train of thought dredged up the memory of a chance encounter that occurred several years ago. I had two little ones at the time, and had taken them to do errands in the busiest section of town. Strapped in the unwieldy double stroller, being pushed down narrow aisles of crowded stores, the two were cranky, hot, and irritable. I was in the paper-goods store when they reached the end of their reserves of patience. My oldest began a full-blown tantrum when I refused to buy him an item that he wanted. The baby howled along in harmony. Both strained to get out of the confines of the stroller.

I was rather cranky, hot, and irritable myself, and knowing that we still had two more stores and a half-hour bus ride ahead of us did nothing to improve my mood. I took my purchases to the checkout counter, and prayed that I could get out of the store quickly.

Someone was ahead of me in line. Her trim suit, custom shaitel, and stylish shoes made me feel downright dowdy. Her manicured hand reached for a beautiful leather wallet in a matching purse, and I wondered why other people always seemed to have it so together. She withdrew the bills she needed, and happened to glance my way. She must have noticed the defeat in my eyes.

"Kids can be tough," she said with genuine sympathy.

"What do you do?" The question burst out before I had a chance to censor the inappropriateness of asking an utter stranger for advice. But there was something about her expression that let me know that she too was a mother, and she too had her share of cranky days.

The woman didn't seem taken aback. In fact, her face took on a serious cast.

"Every week," she replied, "when I light Shabbos candles, I daven for a lot of *koach* and a lot of patience."

She paid for her purchase, and with a quick "Good luck," she walked out of the store and out of my life. But her words stayed with me, and every Shabbos since, I too daven for a lot of *koach* and a lot of patience.

Scissors, markers — all mothers suffer the ravages of the two. All of us have experienced overwhelming days, moments of doubt, and pangs of guilt. There is something comforting in knowing that there are thousands of women out there dealing with the same incident that is facing you at this very moment. So many mothers have handled shorn heads, defaced furniture, and cranky toddlers, and have come out none the worse for wear. This awareness is the glue that binds all mothers together, forming connections between complete strangers.

And on Friday night, as I stand before the glowing lights, I pray not just for me, but for all those wonderful women.

Thumbs and Fries

We all have our secrets, the little habits and foibles we try to hide from the world. My daughter had hers. At five-and-a-half, Devorah was still sucking her thumb. She could only go to sleep if she had the velvety yellow blanket she had received when she was a baby tucked firmly in her left hand. She'd then pop the thumb of that hand into her mouth and drift off while sucking. Every time she stirred in her sleep, the thumb instantly found its way back.

While the thumb was most indispensable at night, it served other purposes as well. I'd always know when Devorah was insulted: no matter how many people were around, the thumb would steal its way towards her mouth, and soon she'd be sucking furiously, turning inwards, shutting out the pain. Interestingly, she also sucked her thumb when she was moved or touched.

Seeing tiny babies made her suck her thumb, as did having a cozy cuddle.

I was worried about Devorah's habit. I had a roommate in seminary who sucked her thumb up until her eighteenth birthday, so I knew how hard the habit was to break. But it was such an important method of self-soothing, such an integral part of her life, that I couldn't imagine weaning her from the habit.

Then I wrote an article about pacifiers.

"You see, Mrs. Gruen," the seasoned orthodontist told me during our interview, "When a child sucks a pacifier, or his thumb for that matter, he perpetuates the infantile tongue thrust. If he's still sucking on something when he gets his second set of teeth, they will inevitable erupt out of alignment. The child will probably also suffer from buck teeth or other cosmetic problems. In the vast majority of cases, he'll need orthodontic treatment, and there may be some speech problems as well."

I dutifully wrote up the article, while my mind raced. The thumb-sucking had to stop. But how? Devorah has remarkably strong will power — when she's sufficiently motivated. What would convince her to give up a habit that saw her through thick and thin? There were few material items she craved. She had desperately wanted a double stroller for her dolls, but we had just given her that as a prize for dressing herself for seven full weeks. No, it would have to be something else.

Then inspiration struck. "Devorah," I said, "remember how you often tell me that you want to go to Yerushalayim alone with me — just me and you?" She nodded, her big gray eyes lighting up. "Well, if you can stop sucking your thumb for a full month, that's thirty days, you and I will go to Yerushalayim together. We'll go to a restaurant, just me and you. Just like big people." The indecision played itself out on her face. First it was touched with euphoric anticipation. Then it clouded over.

"I can't suck my thumb ever?"

"Never. No more thumb-sucking."

"Even at night?"

"Even at night."

Her brow furrowed.

"We'll have so much fun. You can order whatever you want."

Her eyes narrowed. "Anything?"

"Anything."

"But how can I stop sucking my thumb?"

"I'll help you. We'll put band-aids on your thumb so you won't be able to suck it. Want to try?" I did my best to sound nonchalant, pretending that I didn't have much at stake in her final decision.

She nodded, unable to utter the monumental words. We went to the bathroom and put a large band-aid firmly around her left thumb. She went upstairs to play.

Two minute later she was back. "Which restaurant will we go to?"

I hadn't planned this far. "Well, there's Bagel Buffet and Yanky's Bagels. You can get a bagel or lasagna, and they have yummy cookies for dessert." I felt a twinge of guilt — I wouldn't want to be treated to Yanky's Bagel for my special occasion. But then again, I wasn't five years old.

I need not have wasted my guilt. I'd forgotten to take into account that my five-year-old had an eight-year-old sister.

"Menucha told me to ask if we could go to the Sizzling Steakhouse."

Sizzling Steakhouse — that was where my husband and I went on our anniversary. That was where we handed over the credit card and tried not to look at the bill. The place where they charged you for the water you used to wash your hands. A simple meal would run about four times what I was planning to spend on this trip. I rued the day my grandmother treated us

all to dinner at Sizzling Steakhouse. We'd had the most wonderful time, but the meal had introduced my kids to something
beyond pizza shops and greasy schwarma joints. Then again, a
meal at Sizzling Steakhouse would cost far less than two years
of braces.

The gray eyes were watching me. I thought about what she'd
have to give up. I thought about the balance in the bank. I took
a deep breath and said, "If that's where you want to go, that's
where we'll go." Her eyes danced.

After that it was smooth sailing. Devorah would sleep holding
her hand tightly beneath the quilt to keep from sucking. She'd
trap the errant thumb between her fingers when she'd get insulted. She'd wrap her hand around the bar of the bunk bed
when she'd awaken in the middle of the night. She had a single-
minded determination that left me in awe.

A week passed, then another. Devorah never sucked her
thumb. Soon we were counting down the days, then the hours.
I arranged for a babysitter, made a simple supper for the jealous
siblings left behind, and we were off.

I recognized the maître d'. He looked slightly amused to see
my diminutive companion, but he ushered us in graciously. I
scanned the room and selected a small table tucked into the corner of the room. We sat down, and a waiter soon brought us
oversized leather menus. Trying not to break our budget entirely,
I ordered a steak sandwich. After some deliberation, Devorah selected a schnitzel and pastrami sandwich with a side of fries. We
talked in low tones while we waited for the food. Devorah kept
scanning the room, taking in every detail so she could report
back to her friends the next day.

Our meal arrived. Devorah oohed over the parsley sprinkled
on the rim of the plates, and was thrilled at the size of her dish.
We went to wash, and took our first contented bite. I was just

sinking into a feeling of utter well-being when I heard Devorah say, "They're burned."

"What's burned?"

"The French fries. They're burned."

I looked at the offending fries. A bit well-done perhaps. But certainly not burned. I tasted one just to be sure.

"Yum, these are crispy. People love their fries like this."

"But I don't. They're burned."

The same will power that allowed her to stop sucking her thumb cold turkey was asserting itself now.

"Why don't you try one more?"

She did, and then wrinkled her nose. "Don't like them."

I sighed. We were spending a fortune trying to create a dream evening for Devorah. And she wasn't happy. I loathe sending anything back to the kitchen when I eat out. But it didn't look like I had much choice.

I flagged the waiter.

"These fries are really delicious — at least I think so — but my daughter is very sensitive to anything even slightly well-done and she feels that they taste burned."

"Of course, ma'am. No problem at all. I'll bring you a fresh batch."

Five minutes later he returned bearing a plate of golden fries. He placed them in front of Devorah with a flourish. Then he looked over at me.

"She may be little," he told me, "but she's right."

Devorah finished every last fry on the plate, beaming all the while. She'd achieved my goal — no more thumb-sucking, and her goal — a special night out, with perfectly done fries. I watched her with bemused jealousy. If only I could have the same single-minded intensity in achieving my goals. One of which is raising a headstrong little girl who can achieve whatever she puts her mind to ....

To Praise and to Thank

The gaily wrapped package lay unobtrusively on a corner of my kitchen table. I noticed it out of the corner of my eye when I went to order a cab for a member of my weekly class.

"Oh, no," I thought. "Someone forgot this here. I hope whoever left it is still here, so I won't have to make fifteen calls to track her." Before announcing the lost present, I leaned down to take a better look. Pasted on the elegant maroon-and-gold wrapping paper was a small envelope. It had only one word on it — my name. Someone had bought me a gift. I was flattered and surprised.

Courtesy dictated that I wait for everyone to leave before unwrapping the mysterious package. When the last woman closed the door, I opened the envelope. Written in small, perfect handwriting was a short message: "Dear Bassi, Thank you for opening your home to our class. May the *Shechinah* always reside in your home." It was signed by the teacher of the class. Inside the package was a box of beautiful cards.

I stood there in the kitchen, holding the small gift, letting the good feelings wash over me. This wonderful woman, who traveled for an hour-and-a-half each way to reach my home to teach us a class on *shalom bayis*, was thanking me for setting up some chairs and putting out a bottle of water. And she didn't simply express her thanks in words (as she never fails to do each week), but had gone out of her way to buy and wrap a small gift for me before Chanukah. This gesture spoke louder than any class she'd ever given on appreciation and gratitude.

A few minutes later I was struggling into my coat and boots as I headed out to my daughters' school. In a departure from the norm, my older daughter's teacher had invited the parents to a PTA meeting in the morning. And once I was going to the school, I figured it would be the perfect time to discuss my younger daughter's halting Hebrew with her teacher.

My trip went well. My older daughter's teacher was open and attentive, eager to learn all I could tell her about my child. My little one's teacher was equally helpful. She gave me lots of time, discussed the issue at length, and promised to speak with the school language expert. I left feeling accomplished.

An hour-and-a-half after I had left, I was home, back in front of my computer. But something was niggling at my conscience. I was so impressed with the teachers, with their care and concern. In the past, I've had occasion to call the school and complain. Now that I was happy, why not share those feelings, why not express my gratitude? Trying not to feel foolish, I dialed the school's number and asked for the principal. She wasn't available. I asked the secretary if she could give her a message.

"I was just at the school," I related, "and I spoke with two of your teachers. I can't tell you how impressed I was. They are so involved, so eager to hear what's going on and to find out how they can help. It's really special. I also was touched by their outlook on life. Both of them kept stressing that we all need Hashem's help, and expressing their hope that He help us maximize our girls' potential. I left the school, and all I could think of was that I'm so glad my girls are here."

There was a split-second pause on the other end of the line. Then the secretary finally managed to sputter, "That's so nice; the principal will be so happy to hear this." Her reaction made it clear that she didn't spend the majority of her day fielding calls from grateful parents.

I had passed on my *shalom bayis* teacher's gift.

Only moments after I ended my conversation with the school secretary, the phone rang.

"Mrs. Gruen?" asked the male voice on the other end.

"Speaking."

"It's Meir Weiss." Meir Weiss? I quickly flipped through my mental files. Then my heart sank. Meir Weiss was the owner of the publishing house that had been profiled in an article I had written. Rabbi Weiss had been kindly during the interview I had conducted, but very specific about how he had wanted his company portrayed. Had the article upset him? Disappointed him? At least he was calling me and not my editor. In my anxiety, I nearly missed his next words.

"I'm just calling to thank you. We've gotten a number of calls since the article appeared. You said the right things in the right way."

"To thank me?" I croaked in relief.

"One has to do that too," he said lightly. "*Ah freilichin Chanukah*." And with that he hung up. My gift of gratitude had already been returned.

I think about all this as my husband sets up his menorah and I hunt for my mother's latke recipe. "*L'hodos U'lehallel* — To thank and to praise," was the purpose of Chanukah. Gratitude is the very essence of these days.

If there was enough oil for one day, and it lasted for eight, only seven days constituted a miracle. Why then do we celebrate Chanukah for eight days? You'd be hard put to go through a full Chanukah without hearing yet another answer to this age-old question. One that sticks in my mind, year after year, is startling in its simplicity. The extra day is to express our gratitude for the reality that oil burns.

As the Ramban points out regarding the miracles involved in *Yetzias Mitzrayim*, the purpose of open miracles is to sensitize us to the series of endless, hidden miracles that constitute every moment of every day. For each of them we owe gratitude.

Perhaps the best way to begin sensitizing ourselves to our Creator's endless kindness is by expressing our appreciation for the kindness of His creatures. And then the light of Chanukah can illuminate our entire year.

TEVES / טבת

Redefinition

There were three tragedies in Teves. Occurring over a period of hundreds of years, they are seemingly unconnected, but actually stem from the same source. On the eighth day of Teves, Ptolemy, the king of Greece, ordered seventy sages to translate the Torah. On the ninth day of Teves, Ezra HaSofer passed away. On the tenth day of Teves, the Babylonians laid siege to the wall of Yerushalayim, setting the stage for the ultimate destruction of the first Beis Hamikdash.

On the eighth day of Teves, Ptolemy, the king of Greece, ordered seventy sages to translate the Torah. This was a tragedy of great proportions. The Greek king didn't simply want to make the Torah accessible to his countrymen; he wanted to reduce it to just another book on the library shelf — to strip it of its transformative powers. He wanted the shell without the soul.

Ezra and his beis din were the ones who composed many of the tefillos we say. He was also the one who counted the verses, the words, and the letters of the Torah. He personified the appreciation of every nuance of the Torah. When he passed away, we lost some of that power. It was in the year he died that the Greek empire was established.

Yerushalayim had stood as a bastion of holiness. When the Babylonians laid siege to the city, they were attacking that purity. They were attempting to reduce the city to yet another one of the many; to topple it from its exalted status.

Each of these events is the tragedy of the holy becoming mundane. Teves is a month of choice — on which side of the fence will we place ourselves? Is our Yiddishkeit a lifestyle or life itself? It is the month of redefinition — of seeing the tragedy of an empty shell, rejecting it, and embracing the meaning within.

A Decade of Devotion

wo days ago, my brother celebrated the last of his sheva brachos. Next week, my husband and I will be celebrating our tenth wedding anniversary. The contrast between the two life-stages is stark.

My brother and his new wife showed up to every sheva brachos on time, immaculately dressed, and smiling from ear to ear. My family straggled in rather late, slightly sticky from the candies the kids had been sucking during the long bus ride, and trying hard to muster grins while fishing around for bibs.

The young couple sat at the head of the table and looked bashful, as speaker after speaker extolled their many virtues and sang their praises. My husband and I did all we could to keep our four kids quiet. We plied the little ones with food, glared at the older ones when they got overly rambunctious, and, when all else failed, took the whole crew out for a walk.

Shabbos sheva brachos took place in a lovely hotel. Many people commented on the deluxe rooms. My husband and I spent the night stripping first one and then a second bed as our two-year-old battled a horrific stomach bug. At the kiddush, there was pleasant chit-chat and good food. I was busy cleaning the floor after my son was sick yet again, and my husband had to put aside his *tisch bekeshe* for the remainder of the Shabbos.

And yet, I would never want to trade places with my brother. Because for every thing we don't have, be it clean clothing, quiet, or the time to slip out together during a meal, there's something else we do possess.

I may not have much private time with my husband, but as our eyes meet over the writhing body of a five-year-old in the throes of a tantrum, they speak volumes. We no longer have four-hour Friday-night meals, talking until the candles burn out, but as I watch my husband keep the children entertained and inspired at the Shabbos table, I appreciate him in ways I never did then.

My husband doesn't come home to a beautifully set table and a piping hot supper. It can take over an hour until the two of us finish the bath-and-bed routine that I started earlier in the evening, and by the time we sit down, I'm famished and exasperated. Yet, when a little voice calls "I need a drink," and my husband jumps up to get it so I should be able to sit, my frustration is replaced with a deep-seated gratitude. It's been years since we slept for eight uninterrupted hours. But as we stumble out of bed at three in the morning — my husband to one child and I to another — the sense of a shared destiny is palpable.

"Therefore a man should leave his father and his mother, and cleave to his wife, and they will become one," the pasuk tells us.

Rashi adds, "Through the child that they bring into this world." Nothing can bond two people as does the shared act of creation. And even though raising those creatures can stretch relationships to the limits, it can also bring you together in the deepest of ways.

If you let it.

Ironically, the way to succeed is by learning a few tricks from the newlyweds. From their involvement with each other we can learn never to take our spouse for granted. Their obsession with every detail of their mate's life can remind us to ask, "How was your day?" — and wait to hear the answer. Their gushing enthusiasm for each other can serve as a prompt to step back and see all there is to admire in the person with whom we are sharing our lives, to appreciate even the daily actions.

And once in a while it's good to pretend. To send the kids to friends or family, and be, just for a day, a young couple again. To share four-hour meals, to take long walks, to have the time for an uninterrupted conversation, to be just the two of us and not the six of us.

We'll do that, my husband and I, for our anniversary next week. As we sit in a nice restaurant, far from whining toddlers and grubby hands, I'll take a good look at my husband. I'll see the man I stood next to under a chuppah a decade ago. And I'll see the dedicated father of our four children. It's the combined picture that will carry me into the next decade of our marriage, with the same thrill of anticipation that my brother and his new wife share. With the added plus of a decade of devotion behind us.

From *CMV* to *VMC*

Six weeks ago, I didn't feel accomplished if, at the end of an evening, I had managed to make and serve a good supper and give the little ones baths. I wasn't elated if I was able to take my kids to buy shoes. It was no cause for joy if I managed to stay on my feet for eight consecutive hours.

All that has changed. Five weeks ago, I came down with an awful flu. Each night I'd toss and turn, burning up with fever. During the day, I suffered from excruciating headaches and pains in every joint. And the fatigue — there were days I couldn't stand up. After a week of this, I realized that this was no normal flu. A visit to the doctor and a few blood tests confirmed my suspicion. I had CMV — Cytomegalovirus — a herpes virus similar to mono. While it was helpful to have a label for what was going on, it didn't help me feel any better. There is no treatment for CMV.

The first two weeks went by in a haze of misery. I'd drag myself out of bed to do the absolute essentials and then collapse again. Dozens of tasks became my husband's burden, and my sister came over twice a week to help keep the house in order. The slightest activity required monumental effort on my part. Changing a diaper, preparing lunch, pre-treating laundry, were towering mountains that had to be scaled with effort that left me limp.

The next two weeks were slightly better. Although there were many bad days, there were good days too. On good days, I'd be able to get the kids out in the morning and function during the afternoon. The fever and headaches stopped, and I began to get some sleep at night.

This week has been even better. Everyday tasks are suddenly doable. I stocked up on two-weeks' worth of groceries without knocking myself senseless. I can keep working past midnight. I'm even having Shabbos guests.

And it's amazing how exhilarating it is to slowly return to normal. I'm acutely aware of every hour I'm able to keep functioning without the need to fall into bed. I rejoice over the ability to climb the eighty-five stairs separating my street from the one above it. I get a thrill from being able to sit through an entire Shabbos seudah without collapsing on the couch. Health feels so great!

I recently began attending a series of classes on *shalom bayis*. During one class the teacher quoted a sefer (whose name I forgot to write down) saying that man's natural tendency is to notice faults and not positive points. Our attention is naturally drawn to what's wrong, while we ignore what's right. We notice the bag of garbage that hubby left by the front door yet again, but are oblivious to the fact that he got the little ones in pajamas before leaving. We can list every time he didn't hang up his coat, but never notice when it's on the hook.

Clearly, this skewed vision shows up in every relationship we have. "Catch them being good," we're told about our children. But who thinks of going into the playroom and saying, "Wow — you two have been playing nicely for so long. I'm really proud." When peace reigns, we rush around maximizing the free time it affords us, and we only enter the playroom when the shrieks begin to emerge.

My ongoing bout with CMV has given me a dose of VMC (vision much clearer). It seems we humans think that life's on track when everything is hunky-dory. We're feeling energetic and upbeat when the kids are occupying themselves quietly, all our appliances and furniture are working and in excellent condition, and the babysitter shows up early — now that's the way life is supposed to run. But a colicky baby, balky washing machine, or tardy sitter all surprise and irritate us.

If we could only flip the picture, how beautiful life would be. If we expected the minor mishaps and upsets that are a natural part of the mosaic of life, and were pleasantly surprised when everything went just as we had hoped, imagine how many moments of happiness would be ours.

Spreading Warmth

As soon as she woke up, Tzirel could tell the day would be frigid. The tip of her nose was uncomfortably stiff and her toes felt icy, even though they were snuggled under a thick down quilt. She had an urge to curl deeper into her quilt and sleep another hour. But Suri had to leave the house in twenty-five minutes. It's true she was already fifteen, but a child at any age deserves to be sent off to school by her mother.

Tzirel got out of bed. It was even chillier than she had feared. Suri would need a warm, nourishing breakfast if she was to brave this cold. Tzirel dressed quickly, and then knocked on Suri's door until she received a groan in response.

"I'm making that cinnamon oatmeal you like so much," she told her daughter. "Hurry up so you'll have time to eat it."

"Oh Ma, I liked that stuff when I was five. Please don't bother. Did you forget I'm on a diet? There's no way I can touch that stuff."

"Diet, schmiet," Tzirel snorted. "It'll be fine; I'll use skim milk and sweetener." She turned up the heat and went downstairs. She hummed as she looked for the recipe. Tzirel hated the cold, but she loved the coziness it engendered. She loved having the family hunker down in the house instead of running out, scattered in a dozen different directions. She loved making steaming hot cocoa, timing it to be ready just as the kids stepped off the school bus. She loved watching the family gather around the fireplace, each absorbed in his own activity, but drawn together by the magnetic warmth.

Not that there were too many to gather around the fireplace these days. The three boys were all married, raising families of their own, and Suri was rarely home. But the cold still made Tzirel want to draw her children close, much like a hibernating bear. She saw the cold as a deep, black hole waiting to be filled with warmth, to be lit by a fire of love.

Ten minutes later, a steaming bowl of fragrant oatmeal was sitting in front of Suri's place at the table. Five minutes later, Suri slid down the stairs, taking them two at a time. She flew into the kitchen, grabbed an apple and a cucumber from the fridge, and stuffed them into her already bulging backpack. Then she spotted the oatmeal.

"Ma," she wailed, "I told you I can't eat that stuff. It's a carb-free day. This will ruin my day before it even starts."

Tzirel bit her lip and said nothing.

"Sorry," Suri muttered. And then she was gone.

Tzirel slowly picked up the bowl. A thick film was forming on top of the oatmeal. It suddenly looked utterly unappealing. She dumped the contents in the garbage, washed the bowl, and went upstairs to make the beds.

Two hours later, the house was spotless, and Tzirel had both davened and eaten breakfast. It wasn't even ten o'clock. Tzirel wandered into the kitchen, absently lifting a stray crumb off the counter.

She would make a soup, she decided. It would be just the thing to serve Meir and Suri when they came in from the sleet and howling winds. And this time, she'd be sure not to repeat this morning's mistake. She'd make a rich vegetable soup with not a speck of the dreaded carbs. Tzirel started assembling the vegetables she'd need on the counter. Just then the phone rang.

"Tzirel, dahlink, how are you?"

It was Aunt Minna. The simple sound of her voice made something in Tzirel's stomach tie itself into a tight knot that would remain tangled for hours. She took a long, deep breath and managed to sound almost friendly when she said, "Baruch Hashem, Aunt Minna, how are you?"

Tzirel had been sixteen when her mother had died. She and her two younger sisters had made a fierce promise to themselves — they would manage to brave the world on their own, no interference needed. But Aunt Minna, her mother's older sister, seemed unable or unwilling to accept that pledge. She was obsessively concerned with "the poor orphans" and insisted on calling at least once each day to hear how they were doing, what they had eaten, and whether the new cleaning help their father had hired was ironing the clothing properly.

Tzirel's sisters laughed at their aunt's interference, knowing she meant well. Tzirel saw it as an attack on her competence, a subtle message that, try as she might, she never would be able to recreate the home that had been destroyed when a drunk driver slammed his car into her mother. She resented her aunt's phone calls with a vehemence that startled even her, and felt tense hours after she had hung up. But Tzirel was well-bred. She remained ever-cordial, answered each of her aunt's questions, and always remembered to send regards to dear Uncle Shaya.

If Tzirel thought she'd be free of her aunt's prying once she set up her own home, she was mistaken. The phone calls decreased in frequency, but she still had to speak with Aunt Minna at least twice a week. More than thirty years had passed since her aunt began calling, but the knot never failed to make its appearance.

"How is Meir's business? And how are your sweet grandchildren?" The conversation slid along familiar grooves. As she replied, Tzirel cut a mound of vegetables into perfect, tiny cubes.

"I'd love to see you, dahlink," Aunt Minna said. "We live so close to each other, but I never get to see you."

"Yes, Aunt Minna, we really have to get together one of these days ..." and with that vague promise Tzirel drew the conversation to a close.

She could now focus on the recipe. Saute the onion until golden. She'd throw in a clove or two of garlic — it couldn't hurt. Add the vegetables and broth and cook half-an-hour. What did they know about making soup — any Yiddishe mama could tell you that a good soup had to simmer for at least two hours.

The kitchen was soon filled with the wonderful aroma of bubbling soup. The windows steamed over. The warmth was filling the hole.

It was about one o'clock when Suri called. She had a huge algebra test the next day and needed help with the material. She wanted to go straight to Dina's house after school and sleep over.

Tzirel eyed the huge pot of soup. "Why don't the two of you come here? I made a really nice, dietetic soup."

"Dina's mother has a wedding tonight. She said we can study together only if I help her hold down the fort. Please Ma — I'm really desperate."

"Fine, Suri. Do you want me to drive over and bring you your nightgown and toothbrush?"

"Oh, don't worry — I'll just take something from Dina. And thanks for the soup, Ma. I'll have it tomorrow."

Tzirel gently hung up the receiver. Outside the wind howled. The black hole seemed to be swallowing her up. The flames she had lit were being snuffed out before they had a chance to spread their warmth.

Tzirel opened the lid of her pot and stared at the bubbling liquid. Then she found a large Tupperware container. She ladled half the soup into the container. She got a large towel from the linen closet and wrapped the container well. Then she put on her coat and boots and walked outside, carefully holding the steaming container.

It took her only seven minutes to reach Aunt Minna's house — they really did live very close. Tzirel knocked loudly. A long pause, and then "Who is dere?"

"It's me, Aunt Minna, Tzirel."

"My Tzirelah!" There was the metallic sound of three locks being opened, and then the door swung open. Aunt Minna stood there in a faded housecoat, her broad smile turning up every wrinkle on her age-worn face.

"How wonderful to see you, dahlink. What's that package you're holding?"

"It's some vegetable soup I just made. I thought you and Uncle Shaya would enjoy it."

"Ah, soup — that's just what I was dreaming of. I'm sure it'll warm us up good."

And in a flash of clarity, Tzirel realized that they weren't the only ones who would be warmed by the soup.

$\mathcal{L}$ost and $\mathcal{F}$ound

$\mathcal{I}$t is one of the hazards of parenting — finding things in the most unexpected places. There are the more benign finds: peanut butter in the jelly, brass tacks in your son's pant pocket, and cookie crumbs in your bed. Then there are the serious finds: your migraine medication in the kid's doctor kit, those overdue insurance forms under layers of crayon scribbles, and your car keys in the ignition of the toy police car.

It's not just things that you find. It is also situations in which you find yourself. Like facing the enraged mother at the park after your little angel pulled her angel's hair, with no provocation ("It looked like it would bounce so nicely"). Like facing your neighbor after your son picked her prize tulips, the ones she imported from Holland ("I wanted to bring you a bouquet").

There are things you find and things you lose. You lose your nicest sweater after your toddler resets the delicate cycle to hot. You lose your favorite out-of-circulation tape after the baby eats the ribbon inside. You lose your new palm pilot after your daughter immerses it in her bath. You lose your cool, your figure, and your sleep. Some days you think you're losing your mind.

But that's not the whole picture. There are other losses and other finds. You find a scrawled note saying, "I love you," on your pillow. You find your five-year-old singing to the baby. You find riding a Ferris wheel thrilling because little people are beside you. You find that you bake the best chocolate cupcakes, untie knots faster than any mom in the neighborhood, and can make three coins disappear simultaneously. You find love within your heart, tenderness in your manner, and dampness in your eye, which you didn't know existed.

You lose your repulsion of spiders because your son is fascinated by them. You lose your awkwardness at jump rope because you practice with your daughter. You lose your ineptness with machinery because your baby needs an inhalator. You lose that nagging sense of purposelessness that plagued you as an adolescent. For you have found that purpose, found it and much more, in a most unexpected place — within your very home.

Were It Not for Your Torah

*L*ast night I attended a poignantly beautiful event, full of joy, yet laced with an unspoken sorrow. A shul near my house moved from the caravan that had been its home for a decade to a beautiful, spacious new building. The highlight of the *chanukas habayis* was escorting the *Sifrei Torah* from the caravan to their new home. The event had all the trappings of an Israeli *hachnasas Sefer Torah*.

First came two long lines of young boys, dressed in white shirts and dark pants, holding flaming torches aloft. They were followed by a van bedecked with lights, topped with an illuminated crown and playing lively music. Just behind the van was the chuppah with the *Sifrei Torah* to which we are all wed, surrounded by dozens of men, feet lifted in dance, voices lifted in song.

In a prominent spot under the chuppah stood the donor who had enabled the building to progress from dream to reality. Adolfo Shlomo Picciotto held one of the *Sifrei Torah*, his face radiating happiness. A slight man in his seventies, Picciotto exuded aristocracy. But it was his story, rather than his visage, which kept my eyes glued to the Brazilian millionaire.

Picciotto had led a dreamy existence. Born in Brazil to a wealthy and influential Syrian family, Picciotto's real-estate deals were wildly successful, and his businesses spread across the globe. He had a loving wife and four children. His extended family was warm and close-knit, and its members often turned to him for advice. He held a prestigious post in the São Paulo Jewish community. Then, ten years ago, Picciotto's world overturned.

His only son Abramo (Avraham) was home for vacation from his studies in Boston. A week after Succos, drunken thugs kidnaped him as he left the São Paulo synagogue. They demanded an outrageously high ransom. Picciotto paid it in full. But the kidnapers murdered his son. His body was abandoned in a remote area, to be found only two days later. Abramo had been twenty-two years old.

The devastated family flew to Israel to bury their only son. R' Bakshi Doron, the former chief rabbi, was requested to officiate at the funeral. The family then sat shiva in a hotel. When the shiva ended, friends and family flew back to Brazil — all except Picciotto. He couldn't leave the place he had just buried his son, his dreams, his hopes. He decided to remain until after the *shloshim*.

During those difficult days, he'd visit R' Doron and the rabbi would give him comfort and solace. It was during one of those visits that they came up with an idea with which Picciotto could commemorate his son's memory. He would build twenty-two shuls — one for every year of Abramo's tragically short life.

Picciotto lost no time putting his plan into action. He became the savior of shuls — he favored struggling communities in new neighborhoods that had already started construction, but had to stop due to debt. He built shuls all across Israel, as well as two in the States. He's almost completed his goal — the shul in Beitar is the twentieth he has helped build.

So there I was, on a languid summer day, watching this remarkable man rejoice. But for all that there was, I couldn't help but think of what would never be.

Picciotto stood beneath a chuppah clutching a Torah to his heart. And in my mind's eye I thought of another chuppah — the one that would remain forever empty.

At the height of the dancing, the men lifted Picciotto aloft on a chair. And as the singing reached a crescendo around the beaming millionaire, another image flitted across my mind — that of a young groom lifted high on a chair, smiling across the room at his radiant bride.

Picciotto was given the honor of affixing the mezuzah to the shul's beautiful entrance. His voice shook slightly as he made the berachah of *Shehechiyanu*. Was he thinking of the home that would never be built?

Suddenly, scenes from earlier that day rose up unbidden. I'd suffered a disappointment that morning. The letdown was so sharp I could taste it — the acrid, bitter taste of dreams gone up in flames. It came on the heels of several other crises and was so unexpected that I had little reserves in my emotional arsenal to deal with it graciously.

I'm too ashamed to admit the exact words I used, but I said something to my husband to convey the abandonment I felt.

Hashem seemed so very distant. It was intensely difficult to get through the day.

But none of my pain came anywhere close to the agony of losing a child. My disappointments paled into nothingness when set next to the despair of discovering that one's only son will never be seen again. Yet look how this man reacted.

I'll never know what went through his heart and head during those first few days after the murder. But I do know that within a month he had taken his pain and channeled it into glorifying Hashem's Name. Rather than sink into despair, feeling estranged from his Creator, he has dedicated a great deal of his time and money to building shuls in which Hashem will be praised. How? Where did he find the courage, the faith, to do so?

Darkness was falling as the entourage entered the brightly lit shul. I climbed the stairs and peeked down at the magnificent *beis midrash*. The room was dominated by a breathtaking Aron Kodesh. And upon it, in cursive gold lettering was written a pasuk from Tehillim:

"*Lulei soras'cha sha'ashuai, az avaditi b'onyie* — Were not your Torah my joy, then I would have perished in my affliction."

And then I understood.

The details of Picciotto's story are taken from, "The Synagogues of Picciotto," an article by A. Y. Yosefi.

SHEVAT / שבט

Nurturance

Just when it seems that the winter will never end, Shevat arrives with the whisper of new growth. Although there are no visible changes, we know that the sap is rising and the foundation is being laid for the blossoming of spring. Shevat is a tangible proof of our Creator's constant renewal of His creation.

"Ki ha'adam eitz hasadeh," Man is likened to a tree. He too, has chances of constant renewal. Yesterday's failure need not define today's activities. Last week's misery need not extend its tentacles into this week. There is always room to grow, to change, to spread out our branches and sprout new flowers.

The soil that nurtures such change is the Torah. The more deeply we anchor our roots in the life-sustaining soil of the Torah, the more beautiful will be the fruits that our trees will produce.

"Fruit Men" and Memories

Tu B'Shvat.

Usually, simply stating the name of a special day on the Jewish calendar will bring a rush of memories, emotions, and associations. For many, though, Tu B'Shvat draws a blank. Sure, it conjures up pictures of green and brown finger-painted trees on the fridge door, and one can't help but notice the ornate dried-fruit displays at the kosher grocery. But for many, there is little that personalizes the day.

Not for me.

When I think of Tu B'Shvat, I instantly envision the "fruit people" I'd construct with my siblings under my mother's direction.

Each little man was created from no less than fifteen fruits — symbolizing the fifteenth day of Shevat. I think of these pert fellows — round grapefruit bellies, gleaming peach-half heads, coconut hair, raisin eyes, and almond noses — and feel a stir of anticipation.

We'd sit all afternoon, putting together our fruit creations, while popping the juiciest morsels into our mouths. Once the table was covered with plates of fruit people, we would bring one to each neighbor. When my father came home, we would sit down to eat the remaining men in a festive atmosphere. There was always a *Shehechiyanu* to recite, and my parents would teach us which fruit should be eaten first. My father would pour us a bit of wine, and sometimes we would sing.

It's been many-a-year since I sat with my siblings constructing edible people, but the tradition is far from dead. For now, each year, my children and I sit around our kitchen table, surrounded by bags and cans of fruit, peels and pits piling around us, as we bring new people to life. Months before Tu B'Shvat, my children start reminiscing about the fruit fellows and making suggestions for various parts of their anatomy. In our family, Tu B'Shvat is a special day indeed.

————•◦•————

Borrowing potatoes for my cholent one Friday morning, I had a quick chat with my neighbor. She mentioned, with a gleam in her eye, that this Shabbos was a special one. I quickly ran through my mental index. What was going on this week? Ah yes, it was *Parshas Zachor*, the one time a year, save *Yamim Noraim* and Purim, that I actually stepped inside a shul.

Why the excitement? She gave a little laugh. They had started this tradition, she couldn't even remember when, of having four kugels the week of *Parshas Zachor*, one for each letter in the Hebrew word *zachor*. "I'm not always sure I want to make them all," she admitted, "but my kids talk about it for weeks. There's no way I can stop this now." She was silent a moment and then added seriously "It makes the Shabbos really special to them."

I took my potatoes and left, musing over how her four kugels transformed *Parshas Zachor*. It was no longer simply a special *leining* in shul; her family realized it was something to be commemorated and celebrated. My kids' knowledge of *Parshas Zachor* consisted entirely of what they were taught in school, and that wasn't much. Her brood, though — all twelve of them — would never forget the week of *Parshas Zachor*.

———•◦•———

Mention Pesach to a group of women on a park bench. If they ever get past groaning about the cleaning and discussing brands of bleach, they will inevitably enter the realm of recipes. It's amazing how nostalgic they'll soon become. Each one has a favorite; a dish which to her symbolizes the Yom Tov. Crispy matzo and spicy *charoses* are the universal gastronomic symbols of Pesach, but everyone cherishes other dishes as well. It may be the fluffy *kneidlach* their mother prepared, or Grandma Ruth's potato-starch sponge cake. Some wax poetic over their mother's *matzo brei* and others get misty-eyed describing their aunt's borscht.

I, for one, will never forget the Pesach "bagel" my Bubby *a"h* made; a dish so time-consuming it took the better part of a day to prepare, and so delicious it disappeared in moments. Since none of her progeny have her patience in the kitchen, chances are that I will never have the opportunity to taste them again. But that doesn't stop me from drooling at their mere mention. Each Pesach, I close my eyes, and I am a little girl once more, sitting in her blue-and-white kitchen, eating the fragrant, crunchy "bagels."

———•◦•———

They say the way to a man's heart is through his stomach. Could it be that the same avenue will help us reach our children's souls? Perhaps.

This is not to say that food should be the focus of our holidays and we should become "gastronomic Jews". Tu B'Shvat is the day to daven for an *esrog* and appreciate Hashem's bounty. But eating the luscious fruit with which He blessed us is certainly a way to do so. *Parshas Zachor* is about conquering evil on its many levels. But a lavish table may help us appreciate the significance of the Shabbos even more. Yes, Pesach is the time of physical and spiritual freedom, and provides an opportunity to clean our souls, but it is often made tangible and special by the dishes the women in our lives labored so hard to prepare.

There's a power we wield in the kitchen. We can stir up memories, ladle out large helpings of fond associations. The smells and tastes that emerge from our little kingdom will be indelibly impressed upon our family's minds, forever connected with special days in the Jewish calendar, enhancing them immeasurably. It's a mighty thought.

I'm off to stock up on walnuts and dried apricots. I have fruit fellows to prepare, so my children will view Tu B'Shvat with the same joy that I do.

Pipes of Love

"Mommy, come here and look." The insistent voice was calling from the kitchen door. To even turn my head in his direction seemed to require more effort than I could muster. It was the end of a very long day.

I had taken the kids to a large, beautiful park a short distance from our home. Just packing to get out was an operation in itself. The plan was to have a picnic supper at the park. So I cooked early, and then raced around the kitchen trying to think of every conceivable item we would need. I threw everything into three large bags, and tried to get the bags, the stroller, the baby, and the kids into the cab I had ordered.

I was no longer so naïve as to think that I could actually relax in the park, but I didn't expect to lose two of the kids within the first two minutes, as I was unloading the bags. One moment Menucha was holding Shlomi's hand, and they were headed to a nearby slide — the next moment they were gone.

The jungle gym in this park is touted as the largest metal gym in the Middle East. While I'm dubious that it actually deserves that title, it certainly is large. I circled it again and again, scanning the dozens of children playing, climbing, and hanging from its surfaces. Fighting off the sick sensation of a leaden stomach falling toward the floor, I set off for the smaller gym at the other end of the park. "Mommy, Mommy," I heard the little voices in the distance. Dizzy with relief, I hugged them both.

The rest of the afternoon was rather uneventful. All four of the kids became coated in sand; the baby got stuck on top of a slide, afraid to move; Devorah got a big scratch; and Akiva helped build an elaborate castle, complete with a water-filled moat. Supper was a smashing success — only one plate blew away, and only two drinks spilled.

Finally, I gathered my sticky, sweaty, tired crew and schlepped them all to the nearest bus stop. We had been waiting for a quarter-of-an-hour before another bus driver informed us that the bus we needed was no longer running.

By the time we got home, we were all that much more sticky and tired. My husband met us at the door and graciously took over, giving baths and brushing teeth. I set about preparing supper for my husband and me. We had just sunk gratefully into our chairs in front of full plates of steaming food, when he started calling.

"Mommy, I want you to see something." It was eight-year-old Akiva at the door, excitement lacing his voice.

"Is there no end to a day?" I thought in annoyance. "Can I never have just a little quiet; do I not deserve to eat supper in peace?" I tried to stop the stream of negativity flowing through my mind. I willed myself to swivel around to face him.

"No," he said, "don't just look; I want you to come to the hall so I can show you something."

Would he never be satisfied? I was so tired I could scarcely string the words of my refusal into an intelligible sentence. "Just show me from here," I said in a leaden voice. "I can't get up."

He shrugged, but he then proceeded to cup his hands, as though they were wrapped around a rope. "Do you feel it?" he asked. "It's a pipe that's full of my love, and it goes straight to you. Can you feel the flow?"

I could have cried.

He had requested that I get up because he wanted me to see how long his love pipe could be, to show me how it stretched over distances. Through my stubborn refusal, I had contracted the very love which was now warming my guilty heart.

"I feel it," I told him. "It feels wonderful." I put out my arms and we embraced.

It was days before I realized that I had missed the essential point.

My guilt was entirely fueled by the content of his message to me. In reality, his request could have had a dozen other endings. He may have wanted to show me his latest Lego creation, a rock he found in the park, or even the pants I had laid out for him to wear the next day, which he claimed were yucky because the pockets were too small. None of these revelations would have elicited the slightest bit of guilt on my part. My severe pangs of conscience were the sole result of watching my child yearning for connection, and being rebuffed by me.

The secret I had failed to grasp is that just about every request is fueled by a desire for connection — even the complaint about the small-pocketed pants. Sure, he also wants a different pair of pants, or a drink, or admiration for his Lego structure. But underlying that is the primal need each child has to feel loved, acknowledged, and appreciated by the most important adults in his world.

If only I could always hear the words not said. If only I could feel the love as it pulses through invisible pipes. If only they could feel my love as it flows back upon them.

The Littlest Tzaddik

Click. The screen went blank. My article was erased. All the reference sites I was using vanished. My two-and-a-half year old had just turned off my computer's power. "Ooohhhhhhh," a strangled cry of frustration and exasperation escaped my lips.

It was late at night. My husband had been delayed and still wasn't home. I had an article that needed to be finished before I could collapse for the night. My little rascal absolutely refused to go to sleep. And now this!

I was ready to explode, to tell my little boy in no uncertain terms how upset I was at what he had just done.

But I caught myself just in time. Was it really so terrible? Inconvenient, yes. Upsetting, yes. Catastrophic? Hardly. I had to save my strong reactions for the truly important situations. If I get so upset over a flipped computer switch, what will I have left in my arsenal when my child lies or steals or commits any of the other childhood foibles that are truly deserving of a strong reprimand?

I set about getting my computer up and running again. Then, in calm tones, I told my little boy, "Shlomi can't touch the computer. Shlomi is not allowed to press the buttons." Shlomi, who by this time had retreated to the daybed a few feet away from me, realized that he had fallen into disfavor for the moment.

"Didn't touch the button," the little voice claimed.

"Shlomi did touch the button," I replied. "But now he knows it's wrong and he's not going to do it again. Right?"

A pause. Then, "Right. Shlomi is a tzaddik." Another pause. "Maybe."

"Shlomi is a tzaddik," I said. "He tries to do what's right."

Fifteen minutes later, I had found my reference sites and re-typed the lost section of my document. And the littlest tzaddik was fast asleep on the daybed, an angelic expression on the face framed by a halo of golden curls.

Two days later, Shlomi was in the throes of a tantrum. After another late night, he didn't want to get up, but *gan* was starting, and Shlomi had to begin his day. I was davening in the living room, but I heard his high-pitched, hysterical screams. "Don't want to get up. Don't want to get up." A steady thump-thump let me know that he was accompanying his cries with kicks. My husband's futile attempts to reason with an overtired toddler were scarcely audible over the screams.

I had reached *birchos hashachar*. Until recently, I'd allowed myself to be oblivious to the power of *amen*. Then, I read Esther Stern's excellent book, *Just One Word*, and was struck by the importance of this crucial word. Since then, I tried to time my recital of *birchos hashachar* for when my husband's home for breakfast, so he can say *amen* to my berachos. Very often, Shlomi joins in.

I walked into Shlomi's room and began saying the berachos in a very loud voice so my husband could hear me over the ruckus. For the first few berachos, the screams continued unabated. Then there was a startling change. "Don't want to — amen — get up. Don't want — amen — to get up." Even the steady kicking temporarily abated. Despite his frenzy of misery, Shlomi had the discipline to stop himself in order to answer amen. He was able to exercise control over his heated emotions. I was impressed.

Of course, I realize that Shlomi wasn't stopping because he wanted to tap into the enormous spiritual power of amen. In fact, he's completely clueless as to the significance of the word he so faithfully parrots after us a dozen times each day. It was simply the powerful force of habit that allowed him to put the brakes on his tantrum and answer amen to my berachos.

And yet, I was stirred at the potential that lies within my two-year-old. He may not know how admirable his act was, but that didn't make it any less remarkable. There really is a budding tzaddik lying within the plump body splayed across the crib.

Every child is born inherently pure. Most of them have an innate belief in their own goodness. But, as they grow up, they need to check in to confirm this perception. Shlomi is a tzaddik — maybe. When they slip and fall, they turn to us for substantiation of that which their minds wish to believe. Are they still good? Do we still believe in them? They may be two, or ten, or twenty. They may mask the question in a million different ways. But that's what they want to know.

And when we answer that question with a resounding "yes," the confirmation of our belief is usually not long in coming.

I'd Forgotten

I'd forgotten how eight pounds of human being can transform your life.

I'd forgotten the depth of the love and wonder that washes over you when the midwife hands you the tiny human being you've been awaiting for so long.

I'd forgotten the intense gratitude you feel as you study the minute features, exquisite in their perfection; how for the next few days the *pesukim* of your *tefillos* leap out at you full of meaning.

I'd forgotten how long you can sit and stare at a sleeping baby.

I'd forgotten the thrill of watching your older children greet the newest member of your family. The pride you feel as you see the tenderness of the older ones. The concern you feel over the jealousy of the little one whose position has been usurped. The joy you feel over watching your family expand — like the petals of a flower slowly opening.

I'd forgotten how incredibly tired you are after birth, how you wish to crawl into a bed and sleep until next year.

I'd forgotten how erratic a newborn's sleep schedule can be.

I'd forgotten how much happiness a newborn can bring to the whole family; how this slip of a person can touch so many grandparents, aunts, uncles, and cousins.

I'd forgotten how lovely it is to carry your newborn out of the hospital. How the guard coos and the people in the elevator shower you with blessings, and even the sun seems to shine extra brightly.

I'd forgotten how sweet it is to bring a new baby home. How complete you feel when you walk through the door with the baby cradled in your arms, the older ones crowding around, and the crayoned signs gaily decorating the walls.

I'd forgotten how difficult it is to come back to the laundry, the PTA meetings, and the dishes when your body still feels shattered.

I'd forgotten the thrill of the first smile. And the second. And the third.

I'd forgotten how everyone you meet treats the new baby as their own — telling you how to dress her, feed her, and care for her, no matter how many babies you may have raised.

I'd forgotten the delight of rediscovering tiny frilly outfits, dainty lace dresses with matching panties, and miniature pink socks.

I'd forgotten how slippery a wet newborn can be; how giving her a bath feels like trying to scrub a tadpole.

I'd forgotten how loud a newborn can cry, and how she tends to do her loudest crying late at night and just before Shabbos.

I'd forgotten how incredibly kind neighbors are; how they shower you with food and babysitting, until the impossible becomes possible again.

I'd forgotten how wise a two-week-old can look as she peers at you with crystal-clear eyes set in a wizened face.

I'd forgotten how difficult a displaced youngest child can act as he tries to find his new place in the family; how poignant is his search for reassurance that he is still loved and cherished.

I'd forgotten how little you can accomplish while holding a baby, but how that should feel like the greatest accomplishment of all.

I'd forgotten how good food tastes when you didn't have to make it.

I'd forgotten how long it takes to leave the house when you have a newborn in tow; how much time is required to collect diapers, blanket, spare clothing, spare undershirt, and burp cloth, and how the baby will always have a leaky, dirty diaper as your hand is on the front door and your doctor's appointment is in fifteen minutes.

I'd forgotten how very soft a newborn's cheeks are.

I'd forgotten how achy your biceps become from falling asleep while your arm is still wrapped around a nursing newborn.

I'd forgotten the dreamy joy of waking to a new day and finding a tiny human being curled next to you.

I'd forgotten the blissful fragrance of a freshly bathed baby.

I'd forgotten how babies always begin crying just as your husband is about to say a *dvar Torah* at the Shabbos table.

I'd forgotten the wonder of that Friday night when you first light an additional candle for the new light that has entered your life.

I'd forgotten. But how wonderful it is to remember.

Frozen Challah

I had made it. I was finally baking challah once again. The yeast bubbled with the sugar in its little white bowl, while I measured sugar and oil into my mixer. Soon the dough was being kneaded. I leaned close to the mixer and inhaled the slightly sour smell. It smelled heavenly.

A short while later, I was standing before a large bowl of elastic dough. I slowly made the berachah of *hafrashas challah*, lingering over each word. I separated a fistful of dough and whispered the words of the *tefillah* I'd been saying for a decade. An important piece of my life was falling back into place.

When I came down with CMV (a form of mono) a few months ago, something had to go. It was hard enough to keep the kids fed and in clean clothing; anything that wasn't utterly essential was pushed to the side. Challah was one of the sacrifices.

As a single girl, there were many things I promised myself I'd do once I had my own home. But once the dreamed-of-home materialized, many of my vows didn't. Making challah regularly was one of the promises I kept.

Every three to four weeks, I'd lug down my enormous, pink plastic challah bowl, take out my mixer, and make a huge dough. Once it had swelled into a smooth mountain, I'd start braiding. Few things gave me more pleasure in the kitchen than swiftly plaiting the strands and creating a line of proud, plump challahs. They'd rise again, I'd paint them with egg, and pop them in the oven. Soon the house was filled with the tantalizing scent of baking bread. My husband would come home to a kitchen counter covered with golden loaves and a supper of fresh onion rolls. Friday morning, I'd defrost a challah and later heat it on the hot plate. After *hamotzi* there'd be a contented murmur as everyone bit into the warm challahs.

Our comfortable routine continued, week after week, year after year. I davened beside my challah bowl, first for children, then for nachas from those children; next for relief for a teething baby, and then for that baby's success in learning. The only time I ever purchased challah was during the first month after I'd given birth. No matter what was going on in my life, challah was a constant.

Until this year. With the crushing fatigue and horrific headaches that characterized my bout of CMV, making challah was beyond my capability. My husband bought the best challah the grocery offered, and hid the receipt from me. I warmed them on the hotplate and there were still murmurs of contentment on Friday night. But the soul was gone.

Once I started regaining my strength, the first thing I wanted to do was resume my challah baking. But my husband was adamant that wonderful as the mitzvah may be, I was doing no one a favor if I would use up the little energy I had on baking challah. I had to agree with him. So we ate bakery challah week after week.

Finally, I reached the point where the CMV was truly a thing of the past. We bought two cubes of fresh yeast, and once again a heavenly aroma filled my home. Friday night I was tingling with anticipation. This week it would be the work of my hand, the result of my *tefillos*, we'd be biting into — not some mass-produced, machine-made loaf. The men went to shul and I set the table. I put the fish and condiments on a tray. Then I pulled down the cherry-wood-and-silver challah tray my bother had bought years ago. I laid a single matzah upon it, and looked for the challah.

It wasn't on the hot plate. It wasn't on the counter. My challah was still in the freezer! Three months of disrupted routine had caused me to forget to remove it from the freezer when I took out the chicken and knaidlach on Friday morning. I stood stock still in the kitchen, utterly disappointed. Then I ran to the freezer, grabbed the smallest challah I could find, and plunked it on top of the hot-water urn. Looking at the clock, I prayed that the rav would give a particularly long speech between *Kabbalas Shabbos* and Ma'ariv.

It was not to be. The men were home a few minutes later. I instructed my husband to sing a very slow *Shalom Aleichem* as I turned the challah over and over on the urn. But kiddush couldn't be pushed off forever. Soon enough, we were all washing and sitting down. My husband made *hamotzi* and then set about sawing the half-frozen challah. We all valiantly bit in, and chewed and chewed. The flavor was good; it was just so — frozen. I had put so much effort into making these loaves, but a small oversight had clouded my great moment.

How often do I do the same thing in the realm of relationships? I may have spent years cultivating a friendship, but then allow fatigue and the chaos of life with little ones prevent me from picking up the phone and checking in with my friend, and our friendship atrophies. I may have spent the whole afternoon playing with my kids, but then I let frustration get the better of me at bedtime and switch into yelling mode, and they go to sleep upset. I may have gone out of my way to prepare a nice supper for my husband, but one sharp sentence and the effort pales next to the insensitivity. After investing so much effort, isn't it worthwhile to exercise the self-control or exert that last bit of effort necessary to perpetuate that which was already set into motion?

Once you've already made the challah — take a minute to defrost it.

My Mother's Cough

I love my mother's cough.

It's very distinctive. First there is a small intake of breath and then the cough itself, deep and slightly hoarse. It is usually followed immediately by another cough, and then a slight clearing of the throat.

For a little girl, that cough meant security. It meant that the sunshine in my life was in very close proximity. Late at night, tossing in bed, I'd hear that cough along with the tread of the plastic soles on the cloth slippers she loved to wear. Those two noises would tell me that my mother was still up, guarding us from all evils. I'd drift off to sleep, cocooned by that knowledge. When she would go out to do errands, it was often her cough, magnified in the drafty lobby of our apartment building, which would herald her homecoming. She was back, and all was right in the world once more.

When she would lie down for one of her rare naps, the house would seem suspended, biding time until she would awaken. Her cough, heard from the end of the hallway, meant that she was once more among us and life would resume.

I would have thought that as a married woman and a mother of children, that cough would no longer carry such significance for me. Yet every time I hear it, my heart lifts. My mother is near, and the safe, cozy feeling returns.

I was startled one night to hear my mother's cough on an empty street in my neighborhood, far from her home. It took a moment to realize that the cough was mine. I tried coughing again just to be sure. Yes, my cough sounds just like hers. This was a rather unsettling realization. My mother is a rock of stability, and her cough could symbolize safety. It seemed deceptive to have a cough that sounds like hers, like a little girl thinking she is fully grown simply by putting on her mother's high-heeled shoes.

Disconcerting as this discovery was, there was also an element of comfort. I felt like I was carrying around a little bit of my mother. Wherever she may actually be on this planet, all I have to do is cough and a piece of her is there. I mulled this over as I walked home in the cold, damp night.

I got home and shrugged off my coat. I stood still for a moment, appreciating the warmth and quiet of my home. Then I changed into my comfortable clogs and got to work. After finishing the supper dishes and folding two loads of laundry, I headed for my kids' bedrooms to lay out their clothes for the next day. They looked so peaceful, slumbering heaps of innocence. In the girls' room, my five-year-old tossed and turned in her sleep. I straightened her covers and kissed her forehead. As I selected skirts and tops, my throat tickled. I coughed once, and then again. My daughter settled more deeply under her covers.

I was mesmerized. Could it be? Did the thud of my clogs and the sound of my cough let her know that I was near? Dare I contemplate the thought that those sounds calm her with the realization that I will guard her from all evil, and allow her to drift off into a deep sleep?

I will probably never know, but that very thought made me feel so small and so big all at once. I was filled with pride at being part of a chain of those wonderful beings called mothers, and awed by the knowledge of how much I could mean to the little people in my life. Humbled and grateful, I kissed my daughter once more and went off to bed.

ADAR / אדר

Joy

Chazal tell us that Adar is the month of joy. It was in Adar that our entire nation was nearly annihilated. The sword lay upon our necks. Then, in a sudden metamorphosis, our enemy was vanquished, our leader arose, and our lives were restored. The joy was overwhelming in its intensity. Adar is the month in which we are grateful and joyful for the simple yet tremendous gift of life itself.

It is often hard to feel happy about that which we have in great abundance. It would never dawn on us to feel grateful for breathing — unless we had just suffered an asthma attack or been rescued from drowning. Only in the desert does one feel overwhelming joy upon being handed a drink of water. But such an attitude is inherently flawed. Our gratitude should be heightened, not diminished, because of the easy availability of that which we need most.

Our children are a case in point. While they are little, they seem to always be around. How often do we appreciate what a gift each one is? How often do we seize the time we have together, cherish the hours slipping away never to return? Twenty years seem like an eternity, but they pass faster than any of us anticipate. Adar tells us to rejoice in what we already have — to grasp our life and make it all that it can be — including our relationship with our children.

Revealed

*H*e wouldn't eat. Rochel's son turned away from the food she held out, never ceasing to pray together with his friends. Standing at the door of the *beis midrash*, she implored, begged, tried to reason with him; he was just nine, after all, too young to be fasting along with the rest of the nation. But in her heart of hearts she understood him. For if the nation were to be annihilated, he'd never become bar mitzvah, never have the chance to fulfill the mitzvos as an adult. That very thought made her heart constrict in terror, and then she hurried home to beg her Father to spare her young children, her family, her entire nation.

How swiftly this nightmare had come upon them. Just nine years ago, they were enjoying kosher food at Achashverosh's feast, secure and happy in their standing as respected Shushan citizens. Mordechai's warning about the spiritual perils involved in attending the party was the only thing marring their pleasure. But they'd pushed his words out of their minds. Now, they were paying the price.

Rochel's husband, Nachum, had been slow to see the matter in this light. At first, he felt that just as Mordechai had jeopardized their standing by forbidding them to attend the king's party years before, it was his stubborn refusal to bow to Haman that was bringing their destruction. It had taken a number of late-night discussions and her whispered prayers before he was able to view the situation from a spiritual perspective.

"You are the one who is endangering our lives," she had cried. "The longer you resist our need to do teshuvah, the greater the danger we face." Slowly, the truth had penetrated his heart and now he was following Mordechai's every word and sending his three sons to learn and pray with the great sage.

But was it too late? Had their fate already been sealed? Her non-Jewish neighbors certainly seemed to think so — one went so far as to finger his sword every time she passed. Another kept talking about how she would enjoy Rochel's beautiful home once her family no longer inhabited it. Even Esther, the Jewish queen, seemed to have turned against them. News from the palace contained reports of lavish parties she was hosting, at which the sole attendees were the king and his evil advisor. They had looked to her as their last hope, and she was bitterly disappointing them. Prayer and teshuvah were the only options. But was their Father in heaven to be hidden from them forevermore?

Rochel stopped trying to tempt her son with food. Even though it was Pesach, she felt as though she were going through a Yom Kippur more intense than any other. She examined her inner self with a painful scrutiny, she made life-changing resolutions, she spoke to her Creator as she never had before. Late one night, when the only sounds she could hear were the plaintive cries of the young boys in the *beis midrash*, she was startled to find herself thinking that even if she'd never live to see another Pesach, this one was allowing her to complete her mission on earth. But how she hoped she could live by her changes, and not simply die with them.

Two days later, Haman was hanging on a gallows towering over the city streets. Mordechai was welcomed to the palace in his place. The king handed his signet ring to Esther and Mordechai, and letters were sent to all Jews, stating that they would be free to take revenge upon their enemies on the fateful day of the 13th of Adar. The sword had been removed from their necks. They would live, they would serve, they would raise new generations. You could touch the joy and exultation that filled the city streets. The Jews embraced the Torah, and each other, with a passionate commitment. The true King had been revealed in all His glory.

Menucha tightly closed the door of her bedroom. But she couldn't entirely block out the sounds of revelry which filled the city. From the street below wafted snatches of music, off-key singing, and the high-pitched calls of excited children. She smiled, and then, remembering that none of those children were hers, the smile crumpled. She reached for her siddur. The *mishloach manos* were nearly all delivered, the soup was simmering on the fire, and the meat heating up in the oven. She could steal a half-hour.

She began davening Minchah, slowly savoring each word. When she got to "*Shema koleinu*," she closed her eyes and opened her mouth. But nothing emerged. Eight years of pleading for her heart's innermost need had left her frozen. She had asked so many times, begged in so many ways, that the words tasted stale in her mouth.

The images cropped up. Their immaculate home — no pictures on the fridge, no fingerprints on the windows, no toy car to trip over in the living room. Their Shabbos table — the crystal, the china, the refined adult discussion, the scholarly *divrei Torah*. No *parashah* sheets, no stories, no bickering. Their vacations — well-planned, easily executed, and filled with the void of what wasn't.

The doctors claimed there was nothing wrong. They couldn't understand why she and her husband still faced an empty home. There was only one place to turn — but He was hiding His face. Would He remain hidden forever?

A burst of music from the street reminded her of the day. She thought of an evil king, a wicked advisor, and the threat of annihilation. She thought of a sleepless night, a metamorphic party, and a complete turnabout. And the dam broke. She cried as she never had. She examined the parts of her soul where she had never before dared to venture. By the time her husband knocked on the door to tell her that their guests had arrived, she felt as though she had lived through a lifetime of Yom Kippurs.

Ten months later, she was counting the tiniest fingers she had ever seen, stroking the smoothest cheek she had ever felt. She was basking in the blinding light revealed when the mask is removed and the King shows His face.

A Mommy's Fun

"**I**s it fun to be a Mommy?" she asked.

Engrossed in changing a diaper, I didn't fully catch what she said. "What, honey?" I asked absently.

"Mommy …" a long pause. Getting the hint, I looked directly at her. Her wide blue eyes were round with curiosity. "Is it fun to be a mommy?"

"Fun," I said slowly, trying to buy time.

I'd never thought about motherhood in terms of fun. Gratifying, fulfilling, challenging, exhausting. It was lots of things. There was plenty of fun along the way. But was being a mommy fun?

The blue eyes waited.

"Sometimes," I finally answered truthfully.

She gave an imperceptible nod and scampered off to play. I stared after her, wondering what had prompted the question, wondering what she had thought of my response. What had she wanted to hear? Had I let her down in some way by my admission that motherhood was not entirely comprised of fun? I wished I could be one of those exuberant mothers for whom parenting seems to be an endless stream of joyous interactions as they laugh their way through the day. But I'm not. I find mothering a complex mix of emotions, a kaleidoscope of enjoyment and frustration, uplifted happiness and nagging feelings of failure.

I mulled over the question all through the day. Dinnertime passed and I struggled through baths, pajamas, and bedtime in a state that thankfully resembled peace. Running into the girls' bedroom to get a brush, I found my daughter still wrapped in a towel, drawing on her new sketch board, after repeated entreaties to put on pajamas.

"This is the fourth time I'm telling you," I hissed in exasperation. "Get into pajamas."

She gave me a sly smile. "It's not fun to be a mommy now, is it?" she asked.

"No," I replied instantly, "it's not."

She gave another nod and reached for her pajama top.

A cute anecdote to relay to my husband over supper, but again, I felt I'd failed.

So when was it fun? I thought. When could I look into those open eyes and tell her I was having the time of my life? Images arose like bubbles. I saw myself with my husband and four kids in an amusement park we had visited a short while before. The kids were on the Rock 'n Whirl, hair flying, faces upturned to the sun, laughing up a storm. They waved exuberantly each time they passed us. Watching their joy, my heart expanded in happiness. I met my husband's gaze, and knew that he, too, was having lots of fun. That day was particularly memorable for me because it had answered a question I'd harbored for years.

I was ten years old and we were on an outing to the county fair. It was the end of the summer, when the sun was still rich and golden, but the air had a nip to it that I loved. There was endless color wherever I looked: Cheery orange pumpkins, so large I couldn't lift them; sheep and cows, jams and pies, endless exhibitions and stalls. We dawdled in the fun house and raced through the scary house. We tried our hand at throwing a ball into a grinning plastic clown's gaping mouth and at tossing horseshoes. My brother won a stuffed dog. We ran from spot to spot, trying to pack in the good times.

At the end of the day, when we were too tired to try anything else, we piled into the station wagon and began the drive home. It didn't take long for the usual bickering over seats to begin. Trying to distract us, my mother asked each of us what part of the fair had been the most fun. Our fight for the window seat temporarily suspended, we each recounted the highlight of our day.

A sudden thought popped into my head. Turning to my mother, I asked "Ima, did *you* have fun?"

"Oh, yes," she answered without a moment's hesitation.

"But how?" I asked, baffled. "You didn't do a thing."

My mother laughed, a golden, liquid sound.

"I have fun watching all of you have such a good time," she said simply.

I narrowed my eyes with skepticism. Was that really true, or was she giving me the "right answer," the one a mother was supposed to give in such situations? Was it actually possible to have fun simply observing others doing fun things? Didn't you have to be engaged in a fun activity yourself? I was highly suspicious of this reply, honest and instantaneous as it had seemed to be.

It took well over a decade for my suspicions to be laid to rest.

Watching my own children laughing in glee as they whirled past us in the amusement park, I suddenly realized I was probably having an even better time than they were. For when your enjoyment is fueled by the joy of others, it seems to expand into something greater and deeper than personal happiness.

And while county fairs and amusement parks are great big helpings of fun, the good times come in little bite-size packages all through the day. It's sharing your baby's gleeful wonder as he tries to catch soap bubbles. It's reveling in the carefree laughter of your little ones as they pump on the swings, reaching for the sky. It's appreciating a preteen's thrill when he finally beats you in a game of chess. It's even, occasionally, coming into your daughter's room well after her shower, finding her still wrapped in a towel, engrossed in a drawing, and leaning down to take a peek and marveling at her artistic expertise.

Is it fun to be a mommy? Not always, little one. But when the fun comes, it's bigger and better than any fun you've ever had.

Moments of Masquerade

*F*ive o'clock. I'm wearing my cook's costume — a large white apron and high chef's hat — while trying to whip up something nutritious, delicious, and fast. I'm interrupted by the loud arguing going on in the next room.

"But you switched; now that one is mine."

"I did not. I told you I would switch only if you gave me two plain stickers for one shiny one."

"Liar! You said as long as I gave you one big one I could have the shiny one."

"Nuh-uh."

"Uh-huh." The sound of a smack. A piercing shriek. So much for trying to let them work things out on their own and not interfering.

"Mooooooommmmmmmmyyyyyyyyy, he hit me and called me a liar!"

"She scratched me and she's trying to cheat me!"

Out of the apron, into my judge's robes. I find the flowing, black garment with its starched white collar uncomfortable. It seems too large for my frame. I hold up the offending sticker.

"Who was the first person to have this sticker?"

"Me."

"Her, but now it's mine."

This will take some time.

Five-twenty. I've gratefully slipped off the robe and I'm back in my chef's outfit, sautéing onions. The rice is boiling in a second pot and the vegetables are waiting to be chopped for a salad. A bubble of satisfaction rises with the aromas of the food.

A sob bursts the bubble. "Mommy, I was playing on the beds and I fell, and my knee banged into the cash register on the floor, and I got a big boo-boo, and it hurts so much and it's bleeding a lot."

In no time I'm wearing a white coat and a trim nurse's hat. I escort the bruised victim into the bathroom, wash the wound, apply an antiseptic, and let her choose a band-aid. A kiss completes the job.

Something smells too good in the kitchen. Flying in, apron strings flapping behind me, I see a frying pan full of burnt onions. I toss them out, chop another onion, and quickly turn off the rice before it enjoys a similar fate.

Six o'clock. My large apron has been replaced with a cute lacy one and I have a matching cap on my head. This establishment needs a waitress and I've been chosen.

"You didn't give us forks."

"I don't like onions; I want chicken without the onions."

"I'm thirsty; where's the juice?"

These patrons are mighty hard to please. I rush around pouring, serving, cutting. and convincing ("This is a house specialty; have you even tried it?"). I pause just long enough to switch into a maid's uniform so I can throw one load of laundry into the washer and a second into the dryer.

Supper ends. It's bath time.

"Who's ready for a bath?" No response.

"It's time for a bath; let's see who gets into the bathroom first. I put in bubbles." Engrossed in a game, they don't seem to hear a word I say. Time for another uniform, one I wish I wouldn't wear as often as I do. In the crisp blue police shirt, whistle around my neck, and hat placed firmly upon my head, I start barking orders. "In the bathroom, you and you. Now. We're having baths this minute."

When they are finally in the tub, I can toss the cap aside as I watch them play, but I keep the whistle. After all, they still need to come out, get into pajamas, and brush their hair.

Seven-thirty. I grab a tube of lipstick and fix my snood. My husband deserves to come home to a devoted wife. I wipe the gravy off the table, reset it, and put the pots on low flames. I know it will be longer than I'd like until we actually sit down to eat, but I can dream that perhaps today will be different.

Our supper over, I tuck a red pencil behind my ear and sit at the computer, editing the last piece I wrote. I cut, correct, and cut some more. The writer within squeals in protest as she watches some of her favorite phrases go. "Excessive verbiage," the editor snorts. Suitably cowed, the writer simmers down.

A phone call comes in from a distraught friend. She's having trouble with her sister-in-law, doesn't want to involve her husband, but can't deal with the tension. I ditch the pencil and switch into soothing pastels, the best therapist outfit I own. Three-quarters of an hour later, she's considerably calmer, but I'm itching to reclaim the pencil. That article is due tomorrow.

Eleven-thirty. Back in the maid's uniform, I'm washing the dishes, tidying the kitchen. My mind has time to plan. I wonder what to send for *mishloach manos*. I mentally review the costumes in our Purim drawer and try to figure out which ones will fit which child this year. I could probably squeeze the baby into the clown suit, but is the material too thin for the frigid weather we've been having? The sailor suit I spent a fortune on last year should still fit my son. I specifically bought a larger size, but will he agree to wear it a second time?

These kids have just one day a year to put on a solitary costume. When they'll become parents — they will wear scores in the space of just one day.

But at least they are fully aware of who dons the costume they so proudly parade. Whereas I — in the dark of the night, when the robes and the aprons, the caps and the coats are all tucked away — sometimes wonder. So much of my day is spent playing a myriad of roles, am I keeping sight of the woman beneath the costumes?

Almost Wrong

I had a particularly odd day last week. Everything went wrong — almost.

Bright and early, I set off to Yerushalayim hoping to accomplish a number of important things. I needed to pick up a credit card at the bank, speak with a publisher, meet with two fellow writers, and take care of a few errands. At the bus stop, I realized I had forgotten the list of questions for the publisher that I had so painstakingly prepared the night before. I immediately called my husband. He raced out with it — handing it to me standing on the front steps of the bus as it was pulling away from the curb. First problem averted.

It took longer than expected to get to Yerushalayim, and then, due to tremendous traffic, the driver refused to drive up the street I needed. I had to walk farther than expected, and the clock was ticking. I worked on remaining calm.

I arrived at the bank. I had been there just two weeks earlier to pick up the credit card that I desperately needed. At that visit, the teller informed me that they were locked out of their safe. Sure that my Hebrew was causing me to misunderstand, I tried to verify the story — but it turned out that my Hebrew was fine and the staff members were, indeed, locked out of their own safe. I was told to return in an hour. I came back in an hour, then in two hours. The safe was still locked, and they were closing for a two-hour afternoon break. I dawdled in the city far longer than I wanted and came back again. The safe was open, but my credit card was not in it. My branch had apparently not sent the credit card to this bank — even though I had called them twice and they had promised to do so. I had the teller call my branch and ensure that it would be sent out immediately.

Now, I was finally coming to pick it up for the second time. The teller went through the stack of envelopes. Once, twice, with no luck. "It's not here," she told me flatly. Fighting a wave of anger, I decided I would wreck my schedule and go to the first branch. But first, I asked her to call and verify that it was indeed there. She did. It wasn't. I wondered if I should just get on a bus and go back home; this didn't seem to be my day. It was getting closer and closer to the time I was supposed to meet the publisher in another neighborhood. I took a deep breath and asked her to look through the cards one more time. She assured me she didn't have it. I asked her to check. It was there. The very last card in the pile. Gratefully grabbing the card, I tried to untie the million knots in my stomach and raced toward the bus stop.

I arrived at my meeting only five minutes late. But the publisher wasn't there. Nobody knew where he was. He had no cell phone. I sat in the lobby and waited. And waited. I forced myself not to think about my next meeting, which was rapidly approaching. I tried not to think about how important this meeting was to me.

Fifteen minutes, twenty minutes, my nerves were getting tauter and tauter. Twenty-five minutes after we had arranged to meet, he walked in. He was deeply apologetic, and we immediately got down to business. Working quickly, we managed to cover all the topics I had wanted to discuss, despite the truncated length of the meeting. I didn't manage to pop into the grocery next door which carried some hard-to-find items I was hoping to pick up. But we had met and it had gone well. I rushed off to the next meeting.

That meeting was uneventful, save for the fact that it took a full hour longer than expected. Then I got back on a bus to the center of town to do my errands and get home. Starving, I stopped at a popular eatery. I purchased a sandwich, and went to go wash. Placing my rings in my mouth, and balancing several bags on my wrist, I filled the cup. And then my rings slipped, and my diamond fell into the garbage can beneath the sink. Peering at the pile of Styrofoam plates covered with opalescent films of grease and the remains of dozens of lunches, my heart sank. I had ten minutes to do five errands and catch the bus in order to get home in time. Who knows how long it was going to take to paw through this disgusting garbage can to find my ring? I was really having a terrible day.

But as I kept looking at the unappetizing heap in the can, I saw something glint. It was my diamond, halfway down the bin. Very slowly and carefully, I slipped my hand in and retrieved it. My hand didn't even get dirty. I washed, had one bite, and saved the rest for the bus. Then, I dashed around, completed four of my five errands in the ten minutes left, and ran to the bus stop. I caught the last bus to leave the neighborhood before the street was closed for the demonstrations taking place all over the city.

When I got home, I discovered that the watch I had gotten in exchange for the broken umbrella I had returned had a dead battery. But other than that, the day had been successful, although at so many points it had looked like anything but a success. I thought about all the near disasters — the list I had forgotten, the credit card which wasn't there, the publisher who didn't show up, the ring that vanished into a garbage can — and how all the problems had worked out in the end. I couldn't help but wonder — why all the close calls? Why so many wrenching moments of stress? If I wasn't meant to have a terrible day, couldn't my successes have progressed smoothly and uneventfully without my blood pressure being raised several notches?

How many times in life are we oblivious of the salvations we encounter? Some are small — we deposit a check in the bank without knowing that had we not done so on that very day we would have gone into overdraft, with all the hassle that entails. Some are big — we cross a street at a blind curve, and don't notice the bus that came hurtling down the road a millisecond later. Some are enormous — we give birth to a healthy baby with all limbs and organs intact, oblivious to the thousands of things which might have gone wrong and resulted in a severely-deformed child, Heaven Forbid. We go through life experiencing an endless stream of near-misses, a steady flow of blessings in the form of all that doesn't go wrong. And we don't even realize it.

Perhaps Hashem wanted to give me a glimpse behind the curtain, a peek at what could have happened, so I could more fully appreciate that which does go right. When I start realizing what can go awry, I can change my focus. Rather than seeing a day in which everything goes wrong as an anomaly, I can learn that a day in which everything goes right is nothing less than a miracle.

On Joy

$\mathcal{I}$t was one of those days when I couldn't wait to go
to sleep. Not simply because I was exhausted, but
because it seemed that only slumber could end the
persistent flow of minor calamities that was marking
my day. It began when I overslept and my son then missed his
bus. It took the better part of an hour to arrange alternate trans-
portation. My three-year-old had six tantrums in under an hour
that morning; a record even for her. My newly repaired washing
machine was making funny noises, and we had just gotten the
highest electric bill in the history of our marriage. My baby, picking up on my mood, was whiny and clingy. The sky was a leaden
gray.

I moved toward the stereo and mindlessly picked out a cas-
sette. I slid it in and turned it on, hoping to provide a distraction
for the baby. Upbeat wedding music poured into my home. I

looked down at the four-month-old in my hands. The corners of his mouth were lifting into a smile and his eyes were bright. "Easy for him," I thought, "he doesn't have to pay any bills." And yet, inexplicably, I was drawn into his happiness. I found myself lifting my feet and dancing. Clasping his pudgy hand in mine, we whirled together, faster and faster. He laughed in delight.

I gazed at his visage. His mouth was open in an enormous smile; his eyes, two blue wells of shining delight. He was utterly and truly happy. It was the joy of a rising sun, dispelling the darkness and painting a sky in delicate shades. It was a budding blossom, a tender sapling. It was fresh, pure and beautiful. "This is joy, in the most real sense," I thought. "He is happy at this very moment without any other thoughts on his mind. His happiness is not conditional, half-hearted, or lukewarm. He is as fully joyful as a human being can be." I envied him his full-hearted joy, and wished I could obtain it as well.

Several days later, I stumbled across an advertisement for a wedding photographer who offered a viewing of a sample video. It was late at night, and I craved the vicarious excitement of a wedding. I sat and watched clippings from an anonymous couple's momentous night. The breathtaking bride spun in front of the camera, her gown rising up around her in a lacy froth. The mothers were giddy and gracious all at once, the fathers staid and slightly solemn.

Then, the *badeken*. Accompanied by throngs of boisterous friends, the groom approached the woman who would soon become his wife. He lifted the veil over her head. The father of the bride came close and blessed his daughter. He was then followed by the grandfather, a man I had not noticed before in the lively crowds. He must have been close to ninety, a dignified and serious gentleman. His step was erect and his manner humble. He stepped up to his grandchild, lifted his hands, and blessed her for a wonderful future.

I caught a glimpse of his expression and found my cheeks wet. His face radiated pure joy. It was the joy of one who has lived and suffered, and yet stands to watch descendants adding links to a chain stretched far back in time. It was a sunset, splashing vivid streaks upon a darkening sky. It was a joy so genuine and tangible; it shone from amidst the glitter of the wedding.

I watched the rest of the video: the chuppah, the animated dancing, and the *mitzvah tantz*. Yet even as I saw the bride and groom float out of the hall to board a limousine as they set off in life together, the zaidy's face never left my mind's eye.

"That is true joy," I thought. "Once you're at the end of this journey, you can experience the full force of the things which are truly important, without any distractions or diversions. You allow the joy to fill you up and don't let it get drowned out with pettiness." I envied his well-earned happiness, and hoped I would merit it myself.

I couldn't help but notice the polarity of the forms of happiness I had witnessed in the span of several days. There was my baby's freshly minted, single-minded happiness, bubbling up instantaneously. He had nothing to detract from his joy. There was the grandfather's potent, grateful happiness, coming from a place deep within. He allowed nothing to detract from his joy.

And what of me, in middle of the journey called life? Can I not appreciate a noonday sun high on the horizon, strong and powerful? Is a flower unfolding any less beautiful than a bud or fully-open bloom?

The next afternoon was unseasonably warm and I decided to take the kids out to the park. I strapped the baby in his stroller. My two daughters flanked him on either side, and my oldest ran slightly ahead, walking backward to be able to make funny faces at the baby. I looked around me and was keenly aware of the fact that I was surrounded by the four people in whose creation I had taken part. We were together. We were healthy and whole. We loved each other. These thoughts suddenly filled me with a surge of buoyant joy.

I didn't abort it by wondering what to make for supper. I didn't kill it by dwelling on the rip I noticed in my son's new pants. I let it grow and blossom. It filled my entire being until I felt so light I was sure I would lift off the ground and soar to the heavens.

NISSAN / ניסן

Renewal

Nissan — the month of renewal. In the Torah, it is Nissan, not Tishrei, which is counted as the first month. For it was in Nissan that we first become a nation — achieved an identity as the people of Hashem.

Pesach is certainly the most critical event in Nissan. As we know only too well, our job is to eradicate chametz. In order to become true servants of Hashem, we need to get rid of all things inflated. This includes our ego. If it is renewal we want, we have to let go of the weight of our own self-importance.

Children do a remarkable job deflating a mother's ego. Nobody exposes our faults as well as a cranky toddler or a defiant teen. It is also difficult to feel haughty while staring our failures in the face.

The lesson of Nissan is that vanquishing our ego is only the first step. Our mission is to fill up that currently-vacant space with a better self, and to renew our relationships, both with Hashem and with the important people in our lives. When we accomplish that, we become truly liberated.

A Sliver of Silver

Egypt, 2448 (1312 BCE)

Shifra sat in an oasis of calm. She was surrounded by screams of horror, wails of grief. But in her home there was only joy and anticipation. She looked at her firstborn son in amazement. Her Egyptian neighbors had all just lost their eldest child. But she, who lived right beside them, had been spared. Her heart swelled in gratitude.

Around the table sat her husband and children. They were singing Hallel, praising the G-d Who was redeeming His people. Roasted meat lay before them in silver dishes, pieces of the *korban Pesach* they had slaughtered that afternoon. How regal she felt, how noble, how free. It was hard to believe that just last year she had been toiling under the blazing sun, with the overseer's whip cracking upon her back. Nearly all her waking hours were spent building structures that sank into the quicksand as quickly as they were constructed; the few hours left were scarcely enough time to sleep, much less give her family the nurturing they needed.

But now, the tables had been turned. During the past months, the Egyptians had been subjected to a series of plagues unlike anything ever seen. The mighty Nile, which they worshipped as a god, had turned to blood. Frogs had overrun the land, lice had infested the people, wild animals had roamed the streets, the cattle had died. Then boils had erupted upon the Egyptians' skin, a hail of fire encased in ice had fallen, locusts had eaten anything left in the fields, an all-enveloping darkness had fallen upon the land. The climax had occurred tonight, when every firstborn had dropped dead at exactly midnight.

And through all the devastation, the Jews had been untouched, as though living in an impermeable bubble. The same G-d striking the Egyptians so harshly was also protecting the people He had chosen as His nation. Two weeks earlier, He had given them their first commandment, that of sanctifying the moon.

Shifra had been struck with how similar her nation was to that celestial body. Each month it would wane and vanish. But then, just when the darkness of the night seemed never-ending, it would begin to wax, until its light again filled the night sky. Her people were the same; no matter how they were crushed, no matter how many of them were destroyed in the struggle, they rose yet again. For their G-d was protecting them from above.

Germany, 4857 (1097)

The Seder table was the simplest Sara had ever seen. Back in Mainz, she and her family had dined on crystal and china, gold and silver. Her father kept the very best for the *"leil shimurim*

— night of protection" as he had loved to call it. Here, with her distant relatives in a tiny village, there were simple pewter and earthenware; no different from what they used every day. But she couldn't complain. She still had what no one else in her family had been granted — life.

If she closed her eyes, she could see them all: her scholarly father, her gentle mother, her beloved siblings. In that one awful day, they had all been killed at the hands of the bloodthirsty Crusaders. The Jews had fled to the castle of the bishop of Ruthard. They had entrusted him with their colossal fortune and with the lives of their families. He had barricaded them in his castle — but to no avail. The Crusaders had broken the bolts upon the doors and slaughtered all those within. In the city itself, the ordinary citizens had joined the soldiers in killing more than one thousand Jews.

Sara had been away, buying fabric for her father's successful textile business. She had returned to devastation. There was scarcely a minyan left of what had once been one of the most ancient and glorious Jewish communities in Europe. Bereft and alone, she had nearly despaired. Then, she remembered her cousins in the distant countryside. Surely, so far from the cities, they must have been spared.

They had been. And they welcomed her as a daughter. She had soon become indispensable in their large dairy, forestalling the nightmares by falling into bed too exhausted to dream. It was on Shabbos and Yom Tov that the memories would surface and the ache in her heart would threaten to crush her. Nearly a year had gone by since the black day, but this would be her first Pesach without her family.

Hours later, with the candles nearly burned down, and her lids feeling heavy from four cups of wine, she listened to her cousins recite Hallel. They praised the G-d Who had rescued His people from Egypt, Who had split the sea for them, Who had watched over them in every generation. And for the first time that year, in the midst of the pain, Sara felt something else — a mixture of gratitude over her survival and hope for the future. A tiny sliver of silver had appeared upon the blackness.

Yerushalayim, 2007 (5767)

Fraidel looked around the table. How proud Papa would have been. How overwhelmed with wonder at the size of his dynasty. Four generations gathered around the Seder table, scores of people who were all her descendants.

Papa hadn't even merited seeing his children marry. And most of them hadn't — they had been reduced to ashes in Auschwitz before they had reached their teens. From her family of fifteen, only Fraidel had survived the fire that had engulfed the European continent.

After the war, she had used her last bit of strength left to make her way to Israel. There she had met another broken soul, and together they had begun to rebuild all that had been lost. There had been few people at their wedding, no one at the birth of her first son. But by the time that son had gotten married, there had been a dozen siblings to share in the joy.

And now — her breath caught in her throat every time her family was together. Tiny babies, vibrant young mothers, graying men, all had risen with her from the ashes; all were a tangible testimony to a G-d Who has never forsaken His people.

The Seder night slowly wound to a close. A spirited Hallel, a piercing cry of "L'shanah haba'ah," and the men began to dance. Fraidel's heart could hardly contain what she felt. She slipped out onto the porch into the cool night air. And above her, a full silver moon flooded the sky with light.

Dating Daze

"**I**t's going really well," my brother tells me, music in his voice. He's involved in a shidduch and he is reporting to me.

"What did you talk about?" I ask.

"Mainly chinuch," he replies. They see eye-to-eye on so many childrearing issues. They have discussed important topics, reached workable conclusions, and wrapped it all up with a big pink bow. I can't help but marvel at the ease with which one can tackle complicated chinuch problems — provided there are no children involved.

Hours later, my husband and I sit down for our nightly cup of tea. Due either to the Russian blood we inherited from our ancestors or to the pervasive chill in our apartment, we both drink copious amounts of tea during the winter. My favorite cup is the last. Sometime around midnight, we sit in the kitchen to-gether, hands cupped around steaming, oversized beer tankards (the only glass we could find big enough to hold the quantity of tea we like). As we slowly sip, we talk about everything and any-thing — the last fragment of connection before we both collapse exhausted into our beds.

Tonight our talk focuses, as it so often does, around the four neshamahs we are struggling to raise. Menucha's teacher sent home a note — she's been coming late far too often. Waking her up early hasn't helped. Is it time for a contest? For consequenc-es? Should we let the teacher discipline her? Should we revamp bedtimes? Our talk circles as we try to come up with a solution. Soon, we're moving on to other problems. Akiva has been com-plaining about his cheder with increasing frequency. Should we worry? Maybe it's perfectly normal for an almost nine-year-old to complain after a hard day, and we should just empathize and move on. But what if there's a serious issue? Is it worth having another conversation with the taciturn rebbe, who wasn't too forthcoming last time we spoke?

There's the strong desire to give our children the love, the tools, and the boundaries that they need. There's concern over how to give all that in the right doses and at the right times. There's a fear of failures that may extract a price too frightening to contemplate. Long after the teacups are put into the sink and the light turned out, I lie in bed and wonder and worry.

Then I think about my brother and his shidduch. How linear are their conversations. How easily they move from problem to solution. Once, long ago, we were able to do the same. I still remember the date. It was in mid-February, but the weather was balmy. We had decided to go to the Yerushalayim zoo. We walked and talked, marveling in our similarity, rejoicing in the meeting of minds. The zoo is built upon a hill. After an hour or two of walking, we sat down to rest on a bench on the very top of the hill. From our perch we could see the city stretched out far below, the white stones glistening in the bright Mediterranean sun.

My future husband brought up some chinuch issues, and we began a long, earnest discussion. What type of school is best for children? What do they need at home in order to thrive? How does one deal with chutzpah? Right there, with the gargantuan rhinos below us, the ostriches to our right, and the endless blue sky stretched above, we solved the trickiest of childrearing situations. We set a path meant to lead us through the labyrinth of raising little people, figured out the secret ingredients that would create happy, productive *ovdei Hashem*.

Two hours later, my soon-to-be husband asked if he could bring me to meet his grandparents. One week later, he asked me to be his wife. And never did we envision agonizing discussions over hot cups of tea.

Four days my brother calls me late at night. "I'm a chassan!" he cries, the euphoria streaking through the phone line, bringing jubilation to my heart.

The new couple comes for supper. I instantly love the kallah, so refined, so mature, so exactly what my brother needs. She treats my children wonderfully, as my brother always has, and I can't help but think of what excellent parents the two of them will make.

And as I look at them together, filled with the buoyant joy of anticipation of a glorious future, I bless them silently. I daven that they too should soon be sitting together at the kitchen table, debating and deliberating, worrying and wondering, as they try to guide their children. And if they, or we, get really stuck, there's always the bench overlooking the rhinos.

Losing to Gain

My Shlomi had an upsherin this past week. Those long, luxuriant locks of gold are no more; the perfect ringlets forming a soft halo around his face have vanished. He's a big boy now — and if you're not sure, just ask him. He has a yarmulke and tzitzis and a very short haircut which transforms his entire face. His eyes, his dimples, his button nose, everything looks different now that he's parted with his curls.

When my other son, my firstborn, had his upsherin six-and-a-half years ago, there was little room for nostalgia. I thought briefly of the blond curls, saved a lock that I still have deep in a drawer, and then moved on to fitting into the role of mother of the big boy. He was my oldest, and each milestone he passed catapulted me further along the journey of motherhood. I was so busy marveling at how big and mature my little boy had become, I had little time to reflect on what was no more.

But Shlomi is my fourth child. Despite my tiny daughter, he is still my baby. I wanted to hold onto his littleness, to the innocence and beauty of his being two. And nothing proclaims my inability to hold onto any age, or any stage, as much as his haircut and the new-found air of confidence he's adopted.

Just as I'm learning to live with the loss of his locks, I'm losing other things as well. Several weeks ago, inspired by several friends who had done the same, I decided to de-clutter my home. This project goes far beyond discarding broken appliances or giving away the skirt I'll never wear. It entails looking through every item in my home and forcing myself to evaluate it honestly. Do I use it regularly? If not, is it something I'll need in the near future? If not, why am I holding onto it? Even items that are used regularly must be carefully scrutinized. Do I really need ten wooden puzzles? Two "size 12 months" boys' snow suits? Whatever is not necessary is given away, thrown out, or sold.

I've been working on this project slowly and steadily, giving the task several hours of my time, whenever I can spare them. So far, a number of bulging, oversized garbage bags have already been sent to the nearby clothing gemach, to a neighbor of limited means, or earmarked for a friend's upcoming yard sale.

Never did I dream the job would be so difficult. I don't consider myself a particularly materialistic person, but getting rid of all these items is proving to be a real challenge. "Maybe I'll need it one day," a voice within cries, every time something is thrown into one of the cavernous bags. "Maybe I'll be desperate for just that item." "Maybe the kids will suddenly miss that toy." I have to persistently remind myself that getting rid of unnecessary items will give me more space for the things I actually need. The giving away of what I don't use benefits others. There is beauty in simplicity, in a lack of excess.

One of the profound truths of life is that there is little of value that we can gain if we are not willing to lose something in order to obtain it. If I want my son to grow and move closer to fulfilling his potential, I need to accept the loss of his babyhood. If I want my home to be clear and uncluttered, I have to give up non-essential items. If I want to lose weight, I have to give up chocolate-chip cookies.

This principle is true in the emotional and spiritual realms as well. If I want a peaceful marriage, I have to let go of my penchant for winning every argument. If I want a warm relationship with my children, I have to give up my habit of using sarcasm when annoyed. If I want to feel close to my Creator, I have to give up my need for control and put my faith in Him.

At first, all we can see is the loss, and the frightening prospect of having a piece of ourselves missing. But if we keep at our goal, over time we will reach the other side, the place where our loss seems infinitesimal when compared with all we've gained.

Oblivious to
the Music

What would happen if one of the greatest violinists alive, playing on a violin worth several million dollars, was plunked into the culturally sterile environment of a Washington, D.C. metro station at the height of rush hour on a dreary Friday morning? Would anyone stop to listen? Would anyone recognize the genius, the soaring beauty of the playing? Gene Weingarten, a *Washington Post* staff writer, was determined to find out.

The idea was born two years ago, when Weingarten left a crowded metro station and noticed a ragged-looking man playing the keyboard. The musician was quite good, but he was receiving virtually no notice. Looking at the amorphous mass of humanity rushing by, Weingarten felt a surge of anger. The thought crossed his mind that even the greatest of musicians wouldn't be able to touch these rushing creatures. But he decided to test his hypothesis before indicting the public.

The result was an intriguing social experiment. Weingarten approached Joshua Bell, one of the finest classical musicians in the world. Bell, 39, is a consummate violinist who plays before awe-struck crowds across the globe. His instrument is a violin crafted by Antonio Stradivari in 1713, at the end of the Italian master's career. Bell purchased the violin for about 3.5 million dollars. Bell and his violin represent musical mastery at its absolute height.

Bell acquiesced to the request with surprising ease. Finding a venue proved more difficult, as metro laws forbid playing music in public for money, but Weingarten overcame this obstacle when he discovered a station with an indoor arcade owned by a private company. The owner graciously agreed to allow the experiment to take place. The stage was set.

On January 12, 2007, at 7:51 on a Friday morning, Bell, dressed in jeans, a long-sleeved T-shirt, and a Washington Nationals baseball cap, opened his violin case, threw a few dollars in as seed money, and began to play. The pieces he performed were not popular, well-known ditties. They were complex, breathtaking masterpieces that have endured for centuries. Bell put his heart and soul into his music, coaxing pristine, resonant notes from his instrument. He played six pieces in forty-three minutes. During that time, 1,097 people walked by the virtuoso.

Only seven stopped to hear the music for more than a minute.

Twenty-seven tossed in some money while hurrying on.

The rest rushed by obliviously.

Weingarten wrote up the results of his experiment in a detailed article in the April 8 edition of the *Post*, two days before Joshua

Bell accepted the Avery Fisher Prize, the greatest honor a classical musician in America can receive.

The reactions poured in. "This story got the largest and most global response of anything I have ever written, for any publication," remarked Weingarten the next day. Over one thousand comments came from around the globe. More than ten percent of the readers wrote that the article made them cry. Cry for the deadened souls that couldn't stop to appreciate the beauty that surrounded them. Cry for the lost moments, the opportunities that slip through our hands never to return. Cry for the rush of life which sucks up the essence of life itself.

Like the vast majority of readers, I found myself contemplating how I would have reacted had I been at the L'Enfant Plaza station in D.C. on Friday morning, January 12th. Surely, I thought, I would have noticed the brilliant music, even if I was rushing past on my way to work. How could I not have been one of the select few who grasped that this musician, this music, was different?

But I didn't have long to ponder. A pressing doctor's appointment pulled me away from my computer screen. I gathered up my jacket and purse, and raced half a block to catch the next bus.

Rushing down the familiar street, I was surrounded by the tantalizing beauty of spring. To my left, an apple tree was just beginning to bud, the small sapling crowned with a shower of delicate white blossoms. Farther along, a garden boasted irises in full bloom, their deep purple heads nodding in the soft breeze. Above, fluffy clouds raced each other in a blindingly blue sky.

But, in my haste that morning, I saw none of it. I was deaf to the music surrounding me on all sides.

Wait for Me

"Wait, wait for me," my two-year-old plaintively cries. He scrambles up the stairs leading to the park as fast as he can, but his graceful older sisters far outstrip him. They have already climbed the stairs and disappeared around a bend somewhere on top.

"Wait, I'm coming too!" He's nearly in tears now, face sweaty from exertion. In his rush, he misses a stair. He falls and bangs his knee, but he's too focused on his goal to stop and cry. He regains his balance and keeps climbing, begging them to wait.

I stand below, watching, and decide to exercise my maternal prerogative. "Girls," I bellow in a voice half the neighborhood can hear, "wait for Shlomi."

No response.

"GIRRRLLLLLSSS!"

Finally, I hear a reluctant, "What, Mommy?"

"Wait!" I say emphatically, "Shlomi wants to come, too."

"Okay," I can hear the impatience in their voices, "we're waiting. Just tell him to hurry already."

Shlomi is panting with effort, but he finally makes it to the top. I watch with satisfaction as my older daughter takes his hand and walks with him to the park. He's beaming.

He's made it.

My kids occupied for the next few minutes, I walk back into my home and sink into the couch. Maybe I'll actually manage to read a bit on this long Shabbos afternoon before they come trooping back demanding snacks and entertainment.

But instead of my book, it's my son's face I see, strained and pinched. I hear the poignant cry of "Wait!" And it brings me back to another scene.

In retrospect, I can laugh. I was so young at the time that I feared I'd be an old maid for as long as I lived. But at that point, with nearly all my friends married and many of them enjoying the sweet world of motherhood, it didn't seem funny at all. I had fewer dates than I would have liked, and the relationships I did start seemed to end almost before they began. The specter of remaining alone forever kept me tossing at night.

I was in a miserable frame of mind when I went to shul one Friday night. I had been attending *Kabbalas Shabbos* in that particular shul for a number of years. I loved the slow pace and the beautiful singing. Even the view was special; as I looked out the large windows, I could watch the fiery orb of the sun dropping beneath the mountains of Yerushalayim. If I strained my eyes, I could almost see the Shabbos Queen as she slowly descended upon the holiest of cities.

I immersed myself in the words of the ancient prayers, and could feel my body letting go of the worries and fears I carried all week. Shabbos was here.

Then, during the short break between *Kabbalas Shabbos* and Ma'ariv, I spotted her. We'd been friendly in high school, but then I had gone to seminary abroad for several years. We'd completely lost touch with each other, notwithstanding the fact that she lived a mere ten houses away. Now here she was in shul. She looked exactly the same — petite build, pert features, bubbly smile.

Except for one change. There was a smooth, shining sheitel on her head. It gave her that unmistakable aura, an air of maturity and experience that we single folk, no matter how much we'd accomplished, just couldn't seem to muster. Was I just imagining it, or did she stand taller now that she could face the world with someone at her side?

Ma'ariv began and I tried to focus on the words I was saying. After davening finished, as everyone slowly wended their way to the door, I approached my acquaintance.

"Mazel tov," I said warmly. "I see you've gotten married since I saw you last. How wonderful."

She turned to me slowly and gave me a withering look. "You must really be out of it," she said, disdain in her voice. "I'm not only married; I have a little boy."

I struggled to maintain my equilibrium. "Well, then I guess I owe you two mazel tovs. How old is your baby?"

"Five months," she said shortly, "and I'd better be going — he might be hungry." And with that she swept out of shul. I stood staring at her retreating back. Then I slowly walked back to my parents' house.

My mother was rushing to put the last touches on the table. As I helped her set out the fish, I told her about the encounter.

"Life is one big race," I said bitterly, "and all my friends are running, flying across the track, while I can't even get past the starting line."

"Life is not a race," my mother said emphatically. "Each person has his own journey that starts at birth, not at marriage, and our job is to make our journey as meaningful as possible, whatever our circumstances."

Sounded good, but somewhere in my heart was a little girl struggling to climb the stairs, calling out plaintively, "Wait for me!"

———•◦•———

Beside me the baby stirs. I absently rock her infant seat as I readjust my snood. I've made it. Haven't I?

But what of those still trying mightily to ascend the steps? Am I just traipsing along at the top of the climb, oblivious to those straining to reach the summit? What am I doing to make their climb easier?

How do I respond when I hear the pain-filled cry, "Wait, wait for me"?

Eating the Orchids

*E*rev Pesach. Drowning in bleach, Q-tips, and pieces of games that no longer exist, I'm hard-pressed to see far enough into the future to be able to figure out what to make for supper. The Seder which will be taking place just one week from today — the finish line we are all straining to reach with house and mind intact — seems so distant. But then I remember the orchids at my brother-in-law's wedding.

————◦•◦————

Badekens have always been my favorite part of weddings. Although it is at the chuppah that the chassan and kallah become husband and wife, emotions seem to run highest at the *badeken*. For the first time in a week, the two see each other. Their dreams and hopes are reflected in the looks they exchange. A veil is dropped over the kallah's face, and the light in her eyes, the flush on her cheeks, is hidden from sight. The father of the kallah, about to give his daughter to another man, steps forward to bless her. How does one cram a lifetime of hope into one berachah? The father-in-law and grandfather each bless the woman about to build her own home. It's hard to remain dry-eyed at a *badeken*.

Not too long ago, I was at the *badeken* of my future sister-in-law. Standing behind the kallah, I had a clear view of my brother-in-law as he approached her. His face was suffused with a glow I'd never seen before. My eyes were glued to his face, my lips moving in silent prayer, when I felt the baby in my arms wiggle. Pulling my gaze away, I looked down. My son had grabbed a beautiful orchid in one of the twisted glass vase which flanked the bride. He was chewing on the stem.

"Do they spray these things with pesticides?" I wondered nervously, as I tried to gently remove the offending flower from his grasp.

My son is nothing if not determined. The harder I tried to get the flower out of his mouth, the harder he chomped down upon the stem. In a different time and setting, I would simply have firmly removed him from the flowers, paying no heed to the hysterical cries which would result from the action. But I couldn't afford to let my brother-in-law's big moment be shattered by ear-piercing screams.

"Whatever sprays they use, are probably not actually poisonous," I attempted to convince myself. "I'll just give him a drink as soon as this is over, to wash away whatever might be around his mouth." I inched closer to the long-stemmed orchids, studying them, as though I would be able to spot any offensive material on them.

My brother-in-law leaned toward his future wife and whispered something. He gently lifted the veil over her upturned face. All around me, faces were wet. I was trying to give my son my necklace in a vain attempt to distract him.

The bride's father stepped forward, and placed his hands upon her head, praying with a singular intensity. My father-in-law approached her next. I attempted to stick my fingers into the baby's mouth to loosen his grip on the orchids. Would the ceremony never end?

And then it was finally over. With exuberant singing and the clash of drums, my bother-in-law turned around, leaving the hall to prepare for the chuppah. In the hullabaloo that followed, I yanked the baby away, ignored his screams, and headed for the nearest water fountain.

Only twenty minutes later, as I sat in the darkened chuppah hall listening to a rav read the kesubah, did I realize that despite having been a mere three feet from the action, I had utterly missed the *badeken*.

———•◦•———

She looked around the house and sighed with contentment. There was not a single crumb, not the slightest speck of dirt to be found. She let her eyes linger over the freshly cleaned drapes, the scrubbed wooden floors, the gleaming windows. She noted the sparkling chandelier, free of its usual burden of dust, and smiled when she glanced into the kitchen; silver foil and PVC covering every surface. Then, for the first time in a month, she allowed herself to curl up on the couch and close her eyes. The men would be back from shul in a short while, but the Seder table was ready, she was dressed in her new pastel suit, and she could afford a well-deserved rest.

It seemed as if she had just closed her eyes when she heard the sound of their feet crunching the gravel in the driveway, and her youngest son's high-pitched laughter. In a moment, she was on her feet, adjusting her wig, hurrying to remove the wine from the fridge. The house was full at once, her sons, married daughter, and son-in-law all greeting her and settling down. "Kadesh," her husband intoned, and the evening began.

They related an ancient story of an ancient people. They spoke of an oppressed nation living amid depravity and trying to remain holy. They told how the people turned to their G-d and cried for help, and described the remarkable salvation He enacted for them.

And all along she fussed. She ensured that the silver decanter remained full. She kept an eye on the clock so the food would be served at the perfect temperature. She frowned as she noticed dust on a neglected window sill. She dressed the salad, and dished out roast, and poured gravy carefully into a silver gravy boat.

Her husband spoke of the cyclical nature of the Jewish year; of the fact that this holiday was not simply a harbinger of freedom for those enslaved in Egypt, but a continuing chance to break free of personal bonds and limitations. Her sons shared nuggets of wisdom, trying to fathom the inner meaning of the beginning of their People. And she noted that the potato kugel was dry; and the new salad recipe she had gotten from her neighbor's mother was a decided failure.

The night drew to a close. Her husband moved to the couch, where he sat learning, soaking in the last bits of holiness. Her sons helped her clear the table, and then retired. She remained in the kitchen, rinsing the goblets for the next day's meal. And suddenly she realized, that after a month of work, despite having been in the center of all the action, she had completely missed the Seder.

—————•◦•—————

I shake myself from my thoughts and begin scrubbing the high chair legs once more. Perhaps I'd better find that Torah tape I've been meaning to listen to. I don't want to spend the upcoming Seder night eating orchids.

Growth

Iyar lies between two pivotal months. It is wedged between the month of Yetzias Mitzrayim and that of Kabbalas haTorah. What is Iyar's significance? On Rosh Chodesh Iyar, the newly liberated Jewish nation reached Marah. The thirsty people discovered, to their chagrin, that the only available water was bitter. Moshe threw a bitter branch into the water and it miraculously became sweet.

Hashem had an important message for His people. He wanted to show them that while life can appear bitter, with His help, it need not remain that way. We are never truly trapped. There is always some choice we can make.

Something else happened at Marah. Hashem gave His nation three new mitzvos. When it is Torah that serves as our guide, we have the ability to make the right choices and turn bitter into sweet.

This is perhaps the most powerful lesson we can impart to our children — and ourselves. We are not passive players in life; we create reality with every one of our actions. The ability to turn bitter into sweet is the not only a sign of true growth. It is also the key to a fulfilling life.

The Bubble Blower

"More, more!" he yelled in ecstasy. Obligingly, I dipped the wand into the soapy solution and slowly exhaled. The room was filled with shimmering orbs. My two-year-old son clapped his hands in glee, and tried in vain to catch the bubbles bobbing near his head.

"Again," he pleaded.

"One more time," I replied. I felt like a character in a fairy tale; with one breath I could create an enchanted world. This time he succeeded in catching one of the larger bubbles. His pudgy finger touched it, and it popped instantly. I watched his consternation at this turn of events. He frowned as he examined the small, wet puddle on the floor, trying in vain to connect it to the magic that had just been.

Inexplicably, I felt a wave of deep sadness. That bubble seemed to represent my life with my children. It suddenly seemed so transitory, an illusion of achievement where none actually existed.

I had taken a break for a year, between learning a profession and landing a job. This time was dedicated to my kids — my son and baby daughter. I did all I could to make this both quantity and quality time. There were weekly trips to the park, play dates, and shopping excursions. We used crayons, clay and paint, and tried our hand at puzzles. I bought all the age-appropriate toys and read "Little Fish, Little Fish" until I wanted to hide it forever. My son helped me bake, and he sat on the counter next to me as I cooked. It didn't come naturally, but I felt it was what I wanted to do, and there was plenty of pleasure along the way. I hoped that I was helping them grow to be happy and secure adults.

Now the negative voices threatened to engulf.

"They are so little," the first one claimed. "They won't remember a single thing you have done with them. They may enjoy it at the time, but do you really think this will pull them through, when they are struggling with identity issues as teenagers?"

"Don't fool yourself," the next one mocked. "I've seen you lose it; seen you make plenty of mistakes. You hope that all will be forgotten with the passage of time, why should the good times be any different?"

"So many others will influence their lives," a third voice chimed in. "Don't forget that you are just one of many factors in shaping their future."

I struggled for control.

"Enough," the voice of reason finally roared. "What foolishness! A child's relationship with his mother is the most important connection he has with the world, and the early years are the most formative. You took Developmental Psychology. You know that a baby deprived of emotional attention will whither, just as one who is physically malnourished cannot survive. A young child may not remember specifics, but a general feeling of well-being will remain with him forever. What you are doing is crucial to their development."

The other voices suddenly vanished, suitably cowed. I got up and drifted toward the kitchen to make lunch. The matter seemed settled, but a nagging sense of futility remained, tugging at the back of my brain, disturbing my peace.

———•◦•———

A few weeks passed. We were sitting on the floor — my little boy and I — building a Lego tower. My daughter cooed nearby. Like many two-year-olds, my son suffers from LFT (low-frustration tolerance). Normal upsets in life — the wrong spread on his sandwich, his favorite shirt in the laundry, a toy he cannot master — send him on a tailspin from which he has hard time emerging. It's something I've been working on with him. I try to remain calm myself, no matter how hysterical he gets. I discuss the problem with him in simple terms, stressing that while upsetting, these events are not catastrophic. But he is very young, and I didn't seem to be making much headway. Therefore, building Lego towers, while one of his favorite activities, usually involved a fair amount of tears.

That particular day, my son had ignored my sensible suggestion to first build a broad foundation for his tower. I held my breath as I watched him pile little Lego on top of little Lego. The inevitable occurred. While reaching for a Lego man, his elbow knocked into his precarious structure and sent it tumbling down. I held my breath, waiting for the shrieks. They never came. Instead, my son turned to me with a lopsided grin and said, "It's okay," and began to gather the pieces together. I engulfed him in a tight hug. Then I lifted my eyes to thank Hashem for a moment of clarity in a confusing world.

Apparently my bubbles do not pop.

Espresso and Independence

Somehow, while I slept (and did laundry and washed dishes and made dentist appointments), my kids began to grow up. The changes were so subtle, they were lost on me as the days slid by one another like dominos dropping in a row. No child is that different from one day to the next, so the changes since last year, or even last month, often went by undetected.

But there is only so long one can remain oblivious to the fact that her little chicks are fast growing wings and attempting to fly on their own. That process is not so simple for the protective mother bird used to life when her chicks simply sat in the nest and awaited her care.

My eight-year-old, Menucha, started a cooking class a few months back. Unlike the baking class she took two years ago, this wasn't about being handed a lump of dough, rolling it into cookies while eating half the dough, and then bringing the finished product home to a grateful family. This course was meant to give the girls the ability to cook on their own. They learned how to peel, chop vegetables, prepare basic dishes, and most, important in my mind, how to clean up after themselves.

Every Tuesday, Menucha has come home with a fragrant dish and a beaming smile. We've enjoyed her round challahs and roast chicken, her meatballs and potato knishes. But she's never taken the plunge and offered to replicate any of the dishes at home. I didn't have the fortitude to suggest that she do so, but I promised myself that as soon as she would express interest, I'd be supportive and encouraging.

Then, on Friday afternoon, a mere three hours before Shabbos, she had a sudden urge. She decided she wanted to make a potato kugel for the family. I blanched. "Now, three hours before Shabbos?! I have to get the chicken into the oven and clean up the house. You need a shower. This is NOT the time to make kugel." So much for my support and encouragement. I noticed her face crumple, and quickly tried to soften the blow. "You know, honey," I said, "it's a matter of timing. Next time, ask me if you can make kugel on Thursday afternoon, and I'll be happy to help you."

The following Thursday, I was drowning under deadlines, a Shabbos guest, and less help than usual. But when Menucha gave me her winning smile and said, "I'm going to make kugel today, right?" I just gave her a cheery smile in return and said, "Sure."

I decided that I'd give her free rein and foster her independence by allowing her to complete every step of the kugel-making process. I had her find the recipe, and let her read that the first step was peeling a dozen potatoes. Then I counted out twelve potatoes and lay them on the table alongside a peeler and a bowl.

"Here you go," I said. She looked at the potatoes, then back at me.

"I don't really like peeling," she admitted candidly. "Can I go upstairs to jump rope? I'll peel them later."

"Okay," I said.

The potatoes sat on the table all afternoon. I moved them off the table to serve supper. I began to think that perhaps I had been spared. Then Bubby came for a visit.

"You're making potato kugel, Menucha? How wonderful! Do you need some help with these potatoes?" So Bubby peeled while Menucha ate supper.

After supper, Bubby offered to drive everyone to the local toy store to pick out Chanukah presents. All thoughts of kugel flew out the window as the kids struggled into jackets and ran out of the house.

We got home two hours later, happy, exhausted, and laden with packages. On the kitchen table sat a bowl of peeled potatoes. I tried to suppress my shudder at the sight. All I had on the evening's agenda for the kids at this point was teeth-brushing and bedtime, but there was another hurdle to be crossed.

"So what do we do next, Menucha?" She carefully consulted her recipe.

"Three onions," was the reply. Not surprisingly, Menucha didn't like peeling onions either. She hit upon a novel solution. She gave one onion to her five-year-old sister, one to her three-year-old brother, and kept one herself. Soon, three little people were trying valiantly to peel onions by hand. Every flaky bit of peel that was removed ended up either on my kitchen counter or on my floor. I pushed the garbage can in their direction.

"Please," I implored. "Use this." So then the peels ended up on the floor near the garbage can.

Ten minutes later the onions were peeled. I tried not to calculate how many onions I could have peeled in that amount of time. I set up the food processor. Then we hit the next glitch. Menucha couldn't manage to fully close the balky machine. Akiva offered to help her. But once he closed it, he insisted that he feed the potatoes into the chute.

"No," Menucha wailed. "I'm making this kugel." I quickly served my son the supper he had missed and offered to be the food-processor-closer. It took several batches, but finally the vegetables were grated.

Next came the eggs. Devorah called me to help her unzip her dress. Shlomi screamed that he needed the bathroom. "You can do it yourself," I called as I raced out of the kitchen.

I was brushing teeth in the bathroom when Menucha appeared at my side.

"I'm not allowed to check eggs," she reminded me. "I'm not yet twelve."

"Right," I said through gritted teeth. "So I'll do it."

I went to the kitchen and checked her first egg. I popped the rice into the oven to reheat and checked her second egg. I was being paged from the bathroom. The baby was starting to protest the amount of time she had been left in the high chair.

"Hurry," I urged. I checked the third egg. It seemed to take forever for her to crack the fourth. Some distant part of my brain noted the care with which she was opening the egg and how she didn't spill any of it on the counter. But the rest of my brain was sizzling with impatience. A fifth egg, a sixth. I started breading the fish for my husband's supper. The baby's screams were getting louder. Finally, the last egg.

"Just add salt and pepper," I called over my shoulder as I ran out again.

"But I don't know how much," came the plaintive call behind me. I helped her add the salt and pepper. I found a pan for the kugel. I showed her how to oil it. I poured the potato mixture into the pan and slid it into the oven.

There, Menucha had made a potato kugel! I wondered if the price had been worth the results.

Friday night. We finished our soup. I brought out cucumber salad and then served the roast chicken and the potato kugel.

"This kugel was brought to you by a very special person," I announced as I placed it on the table. "Menucha made it all by herself." She tried to hide the grin that split her face, but I caught it. We began eating.

"Wow — this is so good!"

"Unbelievable! This is the best potato kugel I've had in a long time."

"Great job!"

The compliments poured in. And, looking at Menucha's face, I realized I hadn't overpaid.

The following Sunday found Menucha and me at the eye doctor in Yerushalayim. The lines were long, the eye drops stung, and she squirmed through the eye exam. When we finally finished, it was time for a treat. I took her to a nice bagel store nearby. They had a breakfast special — a buttered bagel, an omelet, a salad, and a jumbo coffee. I ordered two. We picked out the type of bagels we wanted and decided which vegetables should be added to our omelet. Then it was time for the drinks. I ordered an espresso for myself.

"Maybe they have orange juice for you?" I wondered out loud to Menucha. She looked at me with pleading eyes.

"I want a coffee just like you. Please." I swallowed hard. A jumbo coffee? At eight years old? I looked down at my daughter. She stood poised by the counter, looking over the selections. Her head reached my chest. She was growing up.

"Make that two," I told the man behind the counter.

A few minutes later we were seated at the cozy round table Menucha had picked out. She carefully cut her omelet and added three packets of sugar to her espresso. We ate in companionable silence for a bit and then started schmoozing about everything and anything. I was nearly finished with my meal when Menucha leaned across the table and looked me in the eye.

"Mommy," she said sincerely, "thank you very, very, very, very, very much." Then she took another long sip of espresso.

Beneath the Bureau

Sometimes, when she lay in bed exhausted but wide awake with worry, when her mind would race thinking about the latest electricity bill, the late camp payment, the roofer who overcharged but did nothing, she'd look over at her tranquilly sleeping husband, and feel a sense of rage.

Adina wasn't prone to rage, and the feeling unsettled her far more than the worry that was her familiar companion. But, as if with a mind of its own, the rage would engulf her in a hot, red wave. Why, oh, why, was she the one who always worried? Why was she lying awake at 3 a.m., heart racing and head pounding, calculating and recalculating, but never managing to get out of debt? Why was she the one who would wake up bleary-eyed and miserable, while Ephraim would rise with energy and good cheer?

The anger would burn within her until her better self forced her to think other thoughts. She'd think about Ephraim's schedule — the second job he took on in the evenings, the work he'd bring home over weekends, the overtime he put in at the office. She'd picture him sitting in his study, poring over the bills and checkbooks, his brow furrowed. She'd remember his worn winter coat, the one he refused to part with because a new one cost too much. And the fire would begin to die down.

Then he'd snore lightly in his sleep, and she'd glance at the luminescent dial on her alarm clock, and once again feel choked. They shared a bank account and lived with the same financial reality, but she felt utterly alone. The worry pecked at her soul and drained her joy, while he remained untouched. While she muttered about the plumber's rates, he mentioned Rosh Hashanah and how their losses and gains had already been decided months before. While she bit her fingernails until there was nothing left to bite, he spoke of their Father above Who gave all they were meant to have and willed all that was.

His faith was rock-solid, unshakeable as the monstrous bureau they had been given as a wedding present and had never been able to move since the movers had set it into place. Goodness knows how many marbles, pacifiers, and safety pins were hidden beneath its clawed legs. She wondered sometimes what she would find if something would ever manage to shake Ephraim's belief that "all that happened was meant to be." Not that she didn't admire him. Not that she didn't acknowledge in the depth of her heart that he was right. But she ached for someone to feel her fear.

Things didn't get better; they got worse. One day the mailman dropped the letter that Adina feared above all. It was from the bank. They regretted to inform Mr. Ephraim Sternfeld that he had defaulted on his mortgage payments for the past six months.

If the sum owed was not paid in full within ninety days, the bank would be forced to foreclose on the house. Adina felt her world going black.

When the kids were in bed and the supper dishes washed, they sat down at the kitchen table with a pile of papers and the small gray calculator Ephraim had been using since high school. They added and subtracted, threw out the camp applications, and re-solved to ask for long-overdue raises from their bosses. But the numbers just didn't add up. After two fruitless hours, Ephraim claimed he was heading to bed — he would deal with this tomor-row with a clear head. The rage welled up inside Adina, but she bit her lip and said nothing.

An hour later, she was tossing in bed while he slept soundly. Two hours later she had finally fallen into a fitful sleep. Then a car alarm went off and awakened the neighbor's golden retriev-er, and the resulting ruckus jolted her awake. She looked over at Ephraim's bed. It was empty. Curious, she slid out of the room. He was not upstairs. Adina tiptoed to the landing.

He was sitting in the living room, hunched over a small *Te-hillim*. His face was turned slightly upward, imploring the Father in Whom he put his faith. In seventeen years of marriage, this was the first time she had seen him cry. Ashamed of trespassing on something so intimate, so pure, Adina soundlessly returned to bed.

She lay there utterly still, her thoughts frozen. She'd discov-ered what lay beneath Ephraim's bureau.

Gardens and Souls

When we bought our apartment in a settlement facing the Judean hills, it came with a fair-sized garden wrapped around it. Looking at the blueprint, I envisioned fragrant flower beds and verdant trees. Reality was somewhat different. The large patch of brown earth, littered with rocks and the rubbish that the contractor had left, hardly seemed worthy of the title "garden." Clearly, it was up to us to create the necessary transformation.

I love gardens. I love the colors, the smells, the lush beauty. My mother has a beautiful, well-tended garden with sweet-smelling fruit trees. She also has a gardener who comes by every few weeks, and she herself devotes some solid time to tending her plants. Gardens, I quickly discovered, require either a lot of time or a lot of money.

We had neither. But I really wanted a garden. One day in the summer, we drove out to the nursery. I craved it all — the perennials and the annuals, the hanging plants and the creepers, fruit trees and a palm. We asked for hardy, inexpensive plants that required little care. The one plant I insisted on was a bougainvillea. I had seen them elsewhere, and had fallen in love with the vibrancy of the leaves and the way the plants seemed to drape themselves around anything at all. We purchased two. The nursery was out of fuchsia — my favorite color of all — so I settled on pink and purple.

"Where will you plant them?" the fellow in the nursery asked.

"Along our twenty-foot fence," I replied.

"Two will do it," he told me. "They'll spread and cover the whole fence."

I glanced at the two small plants, and hoped I didn't look as skeptical as I felt.

We brought them home with our other purchases, and eagerly planted them near the dull fence. They were as tall as my three-year-old son. We fertilized and watered our new acquisitions, but within several months, many of the plants had withered. The bougainvilleas, though, flourished.

By the following summer, they had outstripped my four-year-old and were beginning to flaunt their dramatic leaves. They were spreading in every direction and spilled beauty upon my humble garden. The summer after that, they were almost my height, had peeped into my neighbor's yard, and were actually taking over the fence, just as the fellow in the nursery had predicted.

Today, they tower high above us all and grow in more directions than their trunks can support. They are the first things I see as I walk down the steps from the street to my home. I never get over my wonder; every time I see them, I love them anew.

Comes winter, and the colorful leaves vanish; my garden seems dull and dreary without their beauty. I know spring has arrived when the branches start to bud. First comes the green; I watch and wait for the first glimpse of hot pink. It shows, and my heart sings. And each summer, there are yet new branches reaching to greater heights.

They say that the giants of *mussar* would keep houseplants as a constant reminder of the endless possibilities of growth, and the need for constant nourishment to nurture that growth. The latter point was driven home by our peace plant, tucked in the corner of the living room.

This plant has tender memories for me; my husband traveled an hour each way to the city to obtain it for our fifth anniversary. Despite his deep misgivings about bringing a plant into a home with small children, he purchased it because he knew how much I wanted a plant in that corner, to transform our house into a home. To our pleasant surprise, the peace plant has survived several toddlers and even some rough games of hide-and-go-seek.

I was, therefore, rather devastated to come home from two weeks abroad to discover that my neighbor had forgotten this plant when she watered the others. Its leaves were flat out upon the floor, looking sorry and deprived. I was about to toss the whole thing out, when I realized I had nothing to lose by trying to water it. Every hour for a week, I carefully watered the dead plant. Slowly, the leaves lifted, slowly they straightened. It was inspiring to take part in this rescue mission. I knew all was well when a new bud appeared; life was going on.

I watch my children play on the swing set opposite my bougainvillea. I sit feeding my baby beside the peace plant. And I am struck with the thought that, as the *mussar* greats knew, these tender souls need constant nourishment as well. Affection, love, attention, this is the water my personal buds crave. May I be able to provide it, so they too can stretch higher and higher, reaching for the heavens above.

Eleven Fingers

I was watching her in the bath, my little almost-four-year-old who refuses to be called "little." Using washing cups, old toothbrushes, and a liberal amount of water, she was "baking cakes." Stirring the batter for a chocolate cake with vanilla frosting and colored sprinkles, she informed me that she would make not one, but eleven cakes. She held up her pudgy hands and studied her fingers.

"How many fingers show eleven, Mommy?"

"Well, honey, you only have ten fingers. If you want, you can hold up both hands and then just one finger. That would make eleven."

"No," she was getting frustrated at my denseness. "I want to show eleven all at one time. How do I do that?"

"That's impossible, sweetie; you only have ten fingers. You have to pick a number lower than eleven, or wave your fingers twice."

She sat silent for a moment, digesting this reality of life.

"Do you have eleven fingers, Mommy?"

"No, I have ten just like you." This also elicited a moment of silence. Mommy is built just like me. No extra fingers or spare limbs. Mommy is a mortal human just like the rest of us. How strange.

While my children are perpetually amazed at what I don't know or can't do, I am continually astonished by the things they consider within my realm of possibility. They are surprised that I don't have a detailed explanation for the inner workings of an air conditioner, and that I have no idea how to say *hello* in Greek. They mutter when I tell them I can't lift the bike up three flights of stairs alone, and look vaguely disappointed when I inform them that I can't fix the broken stereo — we will have to bring it to a repairman.

I'm Mommy, and Mommy is supposed to know the answers to any and all homework questions; be able to bake and decorate magnificent cakes, complete with the cream flowers that Dovi's mother makes; and fix everything from broken model airplanes to bruised feelings. While I'm flattered by their endless belief in my abilities, the pleasant feeling dissipates as soon as I remember how few of these feats I can actually accomplish.

You would expect that at some point they would simply give up; realize that I am as fallible as they are — just slightly more skilled — and expect no more. And I'm sure one day they will. But in the meantime, they keep asking, fully expecting me to be capable of wondrous deeds.

The irony of it all is that the acts that in their mind would confer greatness upon me are so far from the ones to which I aspire.

When you are old enough to do triple-digit math in your head, you realize that it's the littlest of things which make the biggest difference. When you are tall enough to reach the top cabinet without standing on a chair, you understand that bigness has nothing to do with weight or height, but everything to do with one's heart and tongue, and how one uses the two.

I recently started to attend a two-year weekly parenting class. The fact that I already took this exact class from this exact teacher several years ago does make me feel a bit like a child who has failed a grade. But the additional fact that over fifty percent of the class is also here for round two, is a comfort. So I sit each Wednesday morning, hearing concepts I know so well I could teach them myself, and implement so little that I need to be regularly inspired.

At a recent class, the teacher was discussing the principle of spending time alone with each child. Every child deserves ten uninterrupted minutes of our time each day, she explained passionately; ten minutes during which all attention is focused exclusively on him/her. How those ten minutes are spent is immaterial — provided the child is enjoying the interaction. It may take the form of playing a board game, baking cookies, or just sitting together in bed and talking.

I had a question: "What if your child has a fascination with military planes and nuclear bombs?" I asked. "My seven-year-old is thrilled if I sit and read him a newspaper article about the weapon situation in Iran, providing I explain what is going on every sentence or so. But there is no interaction, we aren't sharing with each other; it's just me imparting information to him. Is that what these ten minutes should be like?"

"If he likes it and enjoys that time with you, it's perfectly fine," she answered.

"But there is no give-and-take," I protested.

"This isn't about give-and-take," came the wise reply. "It's about give-and-give."

I forgot a good deal of the class before I even reached my home, but I doubt I will ever forget that line. In so many ways, it captured the essence of true parenting.

"It isn't about give-and-take," I remind myself when my six-year-old brings home another note from the teacher complaining of her dreaminess. My children are not here to provide me with nachas; I am here to help them learn to function well in this world. "It's about give-and-give," I tell myself, as my sick baby wakes up for the fourth time in six hours.

"It isn't about give-and-take," I mutter when my children start bickering during an outing I planned for days. "It's about give-and-give," I whisper, when I've just snuggled into a cozy corner of the couch, and a high-pitched voice calls for a drink.

While the little people around me think I'm smart if I know the diet of a turtle, they are oblivious to the wisdom I need to react correctly when they throw their food on the floor. While they consider me strong because I can carry a full case of Coke, they know nothing about the strength involved in speaking quietly when all I want to do is yell. But while they may not know of the struggles behind each act, they feel the repercussions. And their faces tell me when Mommy is "Wonder Woman" in their world.

"It's not about give-and-take; it's about give-and-give." I don't always manage to listen to that inner voice, but on the days I do, it's as though I've magically sprouted an eleventh finger.

Transcendence

The most momentous event in Sivan was our receiving the Torah, which would define us as a People until the end of time.

Torah can serve as the ultimate connector. When two people are striving to keep the same Torah, there is a powerful bond between them. Husband and wife share a vision. Mother and child share a direction.

Two friends share a frame of reference. They are tied together by something above and beyond themselves.

But it is so easy to get sidetracked. When we allow other values and ideals to slip into our world, we often find ourselves at odds with the people we love the most. Even worse, we sometimes find ourselves at odds with the voice within us that speaks to our better self. We, then, have to find our way back, to realign ourselves with the Torah that will give us a life that will transcend the present and lead us to eternity.

To Follow

Anticipation hovers over the camp; a collective holding of breaths as three million people await the greatest moment in the history of their nation. Malka scrubs her family's clothing and cleans their tiny tent in anticipation of the great day. But the true preparations are taking place within her soul.

The day before, she had stood with the entire nation as their leader, Moshe, told them of the Torah that Hashem was offering His people. What it entailed was a great unknown. But she did know that her G-d had saved her from the cruelest of bondages, and then split the sea for the Jews while allowing the waves to crash upon the Egyptians. A mixture of the deepest gratitude and awe had welled up within her heart.

She might not know what she would find within the Torah, what it would demand of her, and how it would change her life. But she did know that there was no better life than one in which she was serving her Creator and Redeemer. Her soul roused, the consent burst forth from her lips. *"Na'aseh v'nishma* — We will do and we will listen," she called out. Astoundingly, at the very same time, the very same cry burst forth from the entire nation.

Angels brought crowns, one for each of the two words they had uttered, and placed them upon the heads of the people. Malka had stood among princes. And now, in just one more day, Hashem was to reveal Himself as He gave them the Torah that would redefine their lives. Her people would stand united in their love and devotion, in their willingness to trust and accept the unknown. They would follow their Maker wherever He may lead them.

Moab, 2793 (967 BCE)

Three women trudge along a dusty path. One is leaving the ashes of the life she once had; the others are leaving the grandeur and glory that was theirs. As they near their destination, the one turns to the two. "Leave me," she implores. "I can offer you nothing. Leave me, and secure your own futures." With tears and an embrace, one turns away. The other steadfastly remains at the older woman's side.

She is going from riches to poverty, from honor to disgrace, from fame to obscurity. But she never looks back. For she is also going from a world of depravity to one of holiness, from a vacuous nation to an elevated one, from a life of emptiness to one of profound meaning.

"Where you go, I'll go, where you sleep, I'll sleep, where you die, I'll die," she proclaims. She knows she may never be able to marry; she realizes she may never be fully accepted by the very nation she is embracing; she understands that she may never rise above her position as a simple beggar. Yet she follows her mother-in-law down the path, following her G-d wherever He may lead her.

Miami, 5767 (2007)

Marcie Bradshaw steadies her hand as she slides her airline ticket across the counter. The agent coolly pecks at her keyboard. "Window or aisle?" she asks. Marcie scarcely hears her.

It is the first time she's leaving the country without the farewell of her parents. Even though Lionel and Linda didn't have a moment to spare, they had never allowed their only daughter to fly without accompanying her to the airport. Their absence screams louder than any of the stormy words they had exchanged with Marcie over the past two weeks.

"You are destroying your life," her father had fumed. "You have the whole world open before you — two degrees from Ivy League colleges, experience with the best law firms in the country, job offers I would have killed for when I was your age. And you're going to Israel?! You're going to hole yourself up in some ultra-Orthodox institution and allow yourself to be brainwashed by a bunch of rabbis? Have you lost your mind?"

Linda had tried to be a bit more tactful. "I know you've been under a lot of pressure these past few years," she murmured. "And it's all right to need to take some time off. But why Israel? We can arrange for you to spend a month at our retreat in Costa Rica or plan a nice jaunt through Europe. Why do something so extreme?"

Marcie had tried. She told them about the gnawing emptiness that so often filled her soul. She told them about the religious people she had met on the campus; about the joy and fulfillment and purpose that they seemed to find in their lives. But Lionel had snorted and Linda had cried. So now Marcie finds herself alone in the airport, winging off to a great unknown with no money and a lot of apprehension.

The flight proves to be the hardest part. Once she arrives, she's surrounded by warmth, purpose, and truth — a truth deeper and more penetrating than any she's ever encountered.

Two weeks after Marcie arrives, the seminary is abuzz preparing for a holiday she never knew existed. Shavuot, the teachers explain, is the day G-d gave the Torah to His nation. The seminary has an all-night learning session that culminates in a walk to the Western Wall for prayer at sunrise.

Ever eager for new experiences, Marcie joins the dozens of girls walking through the quiet streets in the dead of the night. As they near the walls of the Old City, they are joined by hundreds, then thousands of others, all headed for the same destination. They squeeze through narrow alleyways and over ancient cobblestone paths. The crowd continues to swell.

Suddenly, they've arrived. The last remnant of the Holy Temple stands silently before them. The inky black of the night is slowly banished as an orb of gold rises from behind the wall. Groups of young men dance and sing while others sway in prayer. Marcie stays on top of the flight of stairs leading down to the plaza, taking in the scene.

And then she looks up to heaven and whispers a silent prayer. "I still may not know what it is You want from me," she tells her Creator. "But I will find out, and I will follow You wherever it may lead me."

Of Mornings and Marketplaces

"**L**earn well and become a tzaddik and *talmid chacham*," was my mother's parting wish to each one of my six brothers as they set out for cheder every day for years. When my own little boy began cheder, the berachah tripped off my tongue with little thought. As I slipped his briefcase over his arms and steered him toward the door, I uttered the same words I'd heard thousands of times and watched him disappear up the steps.

One particularly rushed morning, after a breathless race helping him get dressed, giving him breakfast, and making and packing his sandwich, all before his bus arrived as 7:42, I was surprised to see him tarrying at the doorway.

"Go, honey," I urged. "It's really late. You'll miss the bus."

"But Mommy," he said, "you didn't tell me to become a tzaddik."

"Learn well," I said, "and become a tzaddik and *talmid chacham*."

He smiled. A quick kiss, and he was gone. I was left by the doorway, startled at how much he took my words to heart, touched at what they meant to him.

-----•-•-•-----

Late last night, as my husband and I sat down to eat our *seudas melaveh malkah*, our conversation meandered between the past Shabbos and the upcoming week.

"Oh," he suddenly said, "something happened one night last week which you'd probably like to hear. I was learning different *midrashim* with Akiva about Shavuos. I read him the pasuk, '*ko tomar l'bais Yaakov*,' and told him that Rashi states that it refers to the women who were the first to be addressed about the giving of the Torah. Before discussing the many answers given to the question regarding the unusual order, I asked him what he thought. 'Because when the *kinderlach* go to cheder,' he told me, 'the mommies tell them to learn well and become a tzaddik and *talmid chacham*.'"

I sat there silent, moved and inspired, realizing yet again the power we women have to touch the big and little men in our lives.

-----•-•-•-----

As Shavuos approaches, it is easy to hear such stories and feel a sense of accomplishment. Through the cooking and laundry, the cleaning and mending, I'm helping my husband and son learn, encouraging their pursuit of the most important thing on earth. But I can't help feeling that such a feeling is only half of the real picture.

Yes, in seminary, and in nearly every pre-Shavuos class I will ever attend, the speaker will quote the famous gemarah: "*Nashim, bameh hen zachyan*" (Women, with what will they merit [*olam haba*])? "What does this mean?" the speaker will query. "Women do mitzvos all the time!" He will go on to explain the utter supremacy of Torah learning; how it stands in a league of its own, and how every person must connect with the men and boys who learn it in order to merit the portion of *olam haba* reserved exclusively for those who spend time immersed in Torah learning.

All of this is true. But I think it can lull me into focusing on Torah as being attainable only through the conduit of the males in our life. We may see it as the province of men, and forget to ask an important question. As Shavuos approaches, and I hunt up my cheesecake recipe and debate the wisdom of attempting blintzes once again, there is something else I wish to ponder.

Reb Yossi used to serve a lavish feast on Shavuos. "If not for this day," he would say, "I'd be just like all the other Yossis in the marketplace." He was tangibly showing his appreciation for the myriad ways in which the Torah had transformed his life.

That comment can be turned around to apply to everyone, even the Yossi in the marketplace. "If not for Torah — I believe I must be asking — what would my life look like right now? How would I spend my day? Relate to my spouse? Educate my children? How would he and they perceive me?"

So much of my life revolves around mitzvos: from keeping a kosher kitchen to having that stunning wool suit checked for shatnez to doing many *chassadim* for my family each hour. I am physically involved in Torah all the time. But does my mind follow my actions? How often do I stop to analyze what the Torah actually means to me? To appreciate the depth, the richness, the meaning it brings into my life? Shavuos provides me with the opportunity to ask these questions, to contemplate the answers, and to come out invigorated from the process.

And the next morning, when I tell my son, "Learn well, and become a tzaddik and *talmid chacham*," I will hopefully have a deeper appreciation of the Torah he'll be learning. And I'll be living.

The Little Things

*J*ust half-an-hour ago, I got back from a PTA meeting in my daughter's school. First on the program was a rav who gave a short speech about the importance of raising our children with joy. Next, the principal spoke. She talked about this year's extracurricular activities, the importance of the dress code, and raising money for a new auditorium. After that, we had a well-known woman speaker. She gave a humorous, down-to-earth discourse on how to build up our children — and ourselves. The last portion of the evening was devoted to meeting the teachers. Luckily, I have only one school-aged daughter, so I didn't have to run from classroom to classroom trying to catch snatches of what each teacher had to say.

I got to hear about the importance of second grade — how the girls pick up the basic skills of learning Chumash, acquire penmanship skills, and learn the foundation of mathematics. I listened to what is expected of them as students, and of us as parents. After the talk, despite the late hour, I remained to ask the teacher a question. Upon learning whose mother I was, she gave me a knowing look.

"We really have to talk," she said.

"Of course," I replied smoothly. "I hope to be in touch some time this week." I smiled, and slid out the door and into the cool night air, hoping nothing betrayed my churning stomach. What did she want?

I got home and tried to reach the psychologist I was supposed to be interviewing that evening — the one I'd been trying to reach for days. He was not at any of the numbers he had given me.

A few minutes later the phone rang. It was the babysitter who was supposed to have come that evening. We had to cancel her at the last moment, due to unforeseen circumstances. I had felt terrible the whole evening just thinking about it. I soon learned that my miserable feelings had been fully justified. She called just to tell me that we had wrecked her evening. She had not attended a wedding and had refused another babysitting job, all because of us. I apologized profusely and offered to pay her, and managed to hang up on decent terms.

So, besides a bone-deep fatigue stemming from the fact that I had slept three hours the previous night due to a miserable two-year-old and a runny nose which made everything seem a bit blurred, I had a leaden heart. The minor frustrations, the small difficulties that litter every day of every life, seemed to be piling up upon each other and burying me beneath their heavy load.

It hadn't been like this when I left the house. While I wouldn't say I had been happy, I certainly hadn't been upset. I tried to rewind the evening and put myself back into the headspace I had inhabited six hours earlier. The little ones and I had baked cookies in the afternoon. Chocolate chip with two chocolate lentils pressed into each one. I had rolled the cookies while the girls enjoyed pressing the lentils into the mounds of dough. Of course, they had bickered over who got to put lentils on more cookies, and who would lick the bowl. But all in all, it had been a pleasant half-hour.

As the cookies baked, I had turned on a music tape. The girls called me into the living room. They had formed a circle together with their two-year-old brother. They were dancing, slowly at first, and then faster and faster until they all fell in a giddy, giggling heap to the floor. The baby thought it was hysterical. He kept trying to pull them down as soon as they began dancing, and his high-pitched, rich laughter rang through the house.

The evening progressed. First supper, which only one kid said was yucky, and the others all liked, and then bath time. My toddler and seven-year-old bathed together. I watched them create fantastic things out of mounds of bubbles, observed my miniature man directing a fleet of boats, and had a nice schmooze with my daughter.

As the hour grew late, I started worrying about my oldest. He should have arrived home a while earlier. He had told me he'd be stopping at the local library to exchange his library book, but normally that didn't take too long. Just when I was reaching for the phone book to look up the number of the library, I heard the blessed squeak of the front door, and in he burst. His eyes were shining.

"I read a whole book just now," he informed me proudly. "It's a book you can't take out of the library, so I just sat there and read it until I finished. And I got to take out another one." He heaved an enormous book upon the table. It was an encyclopedia of animals, with dozens of magnificent pictures. We all gathered around to admire it. My son furrowed his brow as he read the small-print captions beneath the pictures.

Two years ago, this child couldn't read. His quick brain helped him stay afloat in class and caused us to miss the problem for a while, but the brutal truth eventually emerged. We had gone to reading specialists, traveled an hour each way for months to give him vision therapy, and worked our way through two expensive tutors.

The last one had been the answer to our prayers. Slowly, haltingly, my son managed to string letters into words and words into meaningful sentences. Watching him stumble and struggle, my heart had constricted. Reading would always be a burden for him, I was sure. Never would he know the joy of simply losing oneself in the world of a book; never would he read anything for the sheer pleasure of it — the process was simply too tedious for him. As someone who enjoys reading above almost any other pastime, the thought had saddened me. Now, before my eyes, was the splendid evidence of how wrong I had been. We were finally sharing one of my deepest loves.

All this had happened in the two hours before I had put on makeup and a sheitel and flown out the door. So many little joys, so many moments of satisfaction and nachas. Yet I had allowed each one to slide over me. I tasted the sweetness for a moment and then let go, allowing the moment to drop into the pool of the past.

How differently I reacted when my evening become more challenging. Then, I held onto each trouble, chewing the problems until I gagged. I let them pile, one upon the next, until they became a brick wall burying me under their misery.

What a glorious life I would lead if I could switch my approach to each — if I could let the bad times slip away and hold tightly to the wondrous moments that dot every day of every life.

Parallel Journeys

*E*rev Shabbos. Yerushalyim. The streets throb with anticipation. Black-coated men hurry through alleys, rushing to beat the sinking sun. Children, scrubbed and bedecked, shout across courtyards, rock younger siblings to sleep, put away the last of the weekday clutter. Stores are shuttered, vendors silenced, all awaiting the coming of the Queen.

The last bus. An eclectic group joined together by their single-minded focus on reaching their destination quickly.

Rivky sits stiffly beside Menashe, holding his streimel box while he grasps the handle of their small suitcase. They are on their way to visit his parents. Seven months of marriage have still not softened the rough edges of the new relationship. Each time they go to her in-laws, Rivky is tense from the Tuesday her mother-in-law calls with the invitation until she steps onto the bus that will take her back to the tiny rented apartment they call home. And even there, she doesn't truly relax until Sunday morning, when Menashe leaves to work and she can call her best friend Suri to have a heart-to-heart. For Menashe is unfamiliar with the nature of such talks, and he squirms every time she tries to draw him into the labyrinth of her heart.

Rivky stares straight ahead. A couple has just boarded the bus. She's clutching a baby in one hand and the hand of a cranky toddler in another. He's trying to pay the driver while maneuvering two suitcases and a stroller. Four more kids scamper on with them. The children fan out to find seats, while their father expertly makes his way through the aisle and parks his luggage near the exit door. He motions to his wife; he's found a seat for her. She gratefully sinks into the seat, balancing one child on each leg. He leans down and tickles the toddler's chin, eliciting a chuckle. She gives him a look of pure gratitude. He gives her a nearly imperceptible wink. And Rivky aches. Aches for that level of connection. Aches for a relationship in which so much can be said without a single word.

Meira rests her head against the cool window pane, keeping one arm curled around the baby and the other linked through her toddler's arm. She's so tired. There was a time in her life when she rejoiced at Shabbos invitations, welcomed the respite from the endless cooking, relished the change of scenery. A decade of life and a half-dozen children have changed her perspective. Now she likes nothing better than the familiarity of her home, her routine, her bed. She's conquered the twin monsters of cooking and cleaning, learned the shortcuts, and allowed herself to simplify.

But going away is another story. She never ceases to marvel at the sheer quantity of items eight people need for a 26-hour period. She races through the house, tossing ties and yarmulkas, spare outfits and parashah sheets, into an ever-expanding bag.

But there is always the galling knowledge that no matter how long she spends packing, something will remain behind. A pacifier, a favorite blanket, or a pair of slippers will not be there when she desperately needs it, and she'll have to deal with the fallout. And then there are the two bus rides, the fights over the seats, the child who will be sick all over his Shabbos outfit, the headband that will slide off and remain on the floor of the bus. But how often can one refuse one's own mother? So here she was, frazzled and worn-out, mentally compiling her "forgotten" list (tea lights, Shabbos brush, socks for herself in case the room was cold).

To Meira's right, a young seminary girl stands chatting on her cellphone. "So we're on our way to this really amazing family in the Old City. They have, like, fifty guests each week, and they are always looking for seminary girls to help out in the kitchen. And, of course, we get to eat, too." A high-pitched laugh. "So Rachel, and Elana, and I figured it would be a real experience. I'll you let you know all about it after Shabbos." A pause. "No, the Eilat trip is in two weeks time. In the meantime we're working like dogs trying to ace our exams. But at least we're stuffing our heads with something useful. I'd much rather be cramming *Nesivos Shalom* than trying to memorize the capitals of each state — you know what I mean? They say that the Eilat trip is amazing, stunning scenery, although isn't every place here stunning? And the Shabbos after that I'll be at my Aunt Gail's house in Tzfat." Another pause. "Next year? Who knows? I feel like since I got here, I'm different each month. Who know where I'll be next year?"

Meira gazes at the traffic with unseeing eyes. Once that girl was her. Once she too gobbled up life in great, greedy chunks, hungry for every crumb of experience, every spark of inspiration. Once she grew in endless spurts, reaching for the very sky. Where had it all gone? Where was the thirst, the drive, the exuberance? Had she left a piece of herself behind?

Michelle snaps her phone shut with a flourish and drops it in the side pocket of her backpack. She shakes her tawny hair out of her eyes, and bites her lower lip. She can laugh off Sherri's questions now, but sometime soon they'd demand answers. What did she want to do next year? Or, to be more honest, what did she want to do with the rest of her life? For the answer to the first question would predicate the answer to the second. Would she follow the path her parents had mapped out before she even took her first step? Would she go to college, find herself a lucrative profession, and settle into the prosperous middle-class lifestyle her parents led? Or would she follow the whispers of her heart? Turn her dream of a home built of bricks of Torah into reality? Answer the call of this ancient Land that beckoned her to remain forever?

Michelle shifts her bag and glances at the woman seated two rows behind her. A dignified matron who seems to be about sixty, her sheitel is perfectly coiffed, her suit elegant without being showy. She sits with perfect posture, back ramrod-straight, yet she still manages to look feminine and demure. She's conversing in quiet tones with her husband, a saintly-looking man with a silver beard cascading down his frock coat. He shakes his head, a slight frown beneath his beard. She softly makes another point. This time, her husband gives a nod and a slow smile. She returns the smile, and her finely-lined face glows.

Suddenly Michelle is painfully aware of her loud conversation, her slouch, her drooping skirt. More glaring is the uncertainty — of her plans, of her future, of her very essence. She wishes she could bottle this woman's dignity, her timeless grace, her quiet strength. Bottle it and take long draughts every time she loses sight of her own inner nobility.

Raizel absently fingers the heirloom brooch pinned to the lapel of her plum suit. Of course Chaim wouldn't want to unexpectedly visit his elderly mother on Friday night; both mother and son hated anything unplanned. And there would be no time to call her before Shabbos. The second idea was much more to his liking. They'd stop by on their way back from shul Friday night, inform her that they were unexpectedly in the neighborhood since Chaim had been asked to be sandek at the bris of his talmid's son, and set up an official time to visit. Then, on Shabbos day, after Chaim gave a shiur, they would go over together for an hour or so.

There were would be mandelbrot, Earl Grey tea, and perhaps marble cake. There would be delicate china tea cups and dainty conversation. Then she and Chaim would each retreat to their Shabbos afternoon learning, she to *Pirkei Avos*, he to the Gemara he was preparing for his shiur the next day. They'd have rolls and herring and egg salad for *shalosh seudos*. Chaim would go to shul, she'd have the borrowed apartment clean by the time he came home, and they'd make havdalah using the mint leaves and beeswax havdalah candle that Chaim favored. And then they'd return to their weekday routines.

It would be as it always was. And their lives were good. She knew that. But sometimes she felt smothered by the monotony. They seemed frozen in the mold they'd poured four decades before. The children they'd so longed for had never arrived. After twenty-five years of *tefillos* and tears, of doctors and treatments, they'd realized that they'd received their answer. It was *no*. They'd carved fulfilling lives for themselves, reached out to students to stand in for the children that would never be. But though the dream was no longer even a possibility, the dream of the dream had never left her.

A sweet young couple gets up, heading for the exit. She's holding a shtreimel case, he's wheeling a trim overnight bag. A quick glance confirms that the two will soon be parents. The young couple steps off the bus, and Raizy stares after their retreating backs. They are at the cusp of the life she once thought would be hers, a life filled with a kaleidoscope of color, as unpredictable as a baby's sleep patterns and a teen's moods. She wants to reach out and touch that color, gather it up, and sprinkle it in her own life.

The sun is sinking ever closer to the horizon, the hush of the streets palpable. In less than an hour the Queen will sweep through her cherished city. And on this holy day, each person will be granted the ability to see their lives afresh. To see it for what it is and not for what it isn't.

The Stolen Hour

*T*hey were stealing the only hour in the entire week that was mine.

That's the way I felt that Friday night a short while ago, when mini-disasters kept cropping up faster than we could deal with them.

Working from home has definite advantages. But it also means you are always at work. When I gave up my office job and started working from the house, my occasional evening in bed with a good book or curled up on the couch catching up with a friend over the phone, suddenly vanished. There was always something I should be doing. Only Shabbos remained my oasis of tranquility, untouched by the computer or phone.

On Friday night, once the table was cleared and the kids put to bed, I'd change into a robe, get a stack of reading material, a hot tea, and some chocolates, and pass an hour in pure bliss. No matter how tired I was, I'd force myself to stay up, explaining to my baffled husband that one can only enjoy relaxing when awake; the state of sleep is one of no awareness. It was a luxurious hour that was all mine.

One Friday night, just before I settled into the corner of the couch, I heard an ominous coughing and then a plaintive "Mommy." I raced to the bedroom, but both I and my three-year-old were too late. She had thrown up all over herself and my husband's bed. She had seemed lethargic during the meal and had complained of a bellyache. When she asked to sleep in our room, my husband settled her in his bed, in the linen I had changed Friday afternoon. Now, that little bit of TLC was costing more than expected. My husband changed her and washed her as best as he could, while I stripped the linen and cleaned the floor. We gave her a drink and a bucket by her bed. A hug and goodnight kiss, and peace was restored.

We went back to the living room, my husband to his Chumash, and I to my book. We both read for a bit. My husband prepared two steaming mugs of tea. I made some comment about the beauty of the quiet.

My observation was premature. A sudden, hysterical scream from the boys' room alerted us to the fact that my baby's ear infection was still not gone, despite his beginning antibiotics. Nights were when the pain would plague him. I looked longingly at the tea, and got up to feed him. My husband gave him some painkiller.

He was just settling down, and I was hoping to reach the tea before it cooled off entirely, when the coughing, gagging noise returned. I unceremoniously dumped the baby in his crib and raced to the girls' room. My daughter was not in bed. She had made it to the bathroom, but not quite far enough. Both she and the bathroom were in a bad state. The baby was screaming his protest of my sudden abandonment. My husband came down the hall and sized up the situation in a moment. Our eyes locked. Despite the inappropriateness of the reaction, we simultaneously burst into laughter. "Better laugh than cry" has always been our motto. Then we got to work.

This time, he cleaned the floor while I dealt with our sick daughter. She said her stomach still hurt. I held her hair out of her face, pressed a cool hand against her forehead, and stood with her by the toilet. I held her tight while she emptied her stomach, then rinsed off her face and began to gently change her pajamas. She looked up, still in a haze of sleep, and the trust I saw in her eyes scared me. It was a look of vulnerability laced with certainty. She was having a rough night, but she counted on me. Counted on me to care for her, tend to her, love her.

As a teenager, I had prided myself on my analytic, almost masculine mind. I was a cool, detached observer of life, never hysterical, nearly always in control. Unlike many of the women around me, I didn't get gushy and effusive, emotional and demonstrative. It seemed like a fine state as a single woman, but as a mother, I had my doubts about my credentials.

I remember holding my firstborn several hours after birth. I stared at the tiny bundle of human being. Clear eyes in a wizened face looked back at me. I was worried. I wasn't feeling an overwhelming rush of maternal love. While enchanted and enthralled by this new life, I wondered how much I truly felt for him. Would I be willing to give my life for him? I squirmed when the answer was not an instantaneous yes.

At some point, I stopped contemplating, and started feeding, burping, changing, and rocking this little person. And the love began to bubble up. Would I place my body over his if we were ever caught in a terrorist attack? I hoped never to learn the answer to a question so horrific, but I was quickly learning that our emotions are sometimes far ahead of our brains.

And here I was, with a sick, smelly, little girl, telling her it would be all right, washing her down, cuddling her on my lap, as I held a cup to her lips. My analytical brain looked on and sneered, "You?! It is other mothers who are soft-spoken and soothing, who give of themselves fully and unconditionally. They are a comforting balm for their children. But you?" And yet, my heart felt just right. Fighting the sense of being a fake, and despite the frustration over my stolen hour, I truly felt loving and tender. And one more look at my little girl told me all I needed to know. Whatever I may think of my mothering, in her eyes, I was the Rock of Gibraltar, a shelter in the storm. She counted on me completely and unreservedly. We sat together for some time while she recovered from her ordeal. Then I tucked her in and gave her a last kiss.

I made my way back to the couch. The tea was stone-cold, I was no longer in the mood for chocolate, and I was so tired my eyes refused to focus on the words I attempted to read.

My beloved hour had been stolen.

But I had received so much more in return.

TAMMUZ / תמוז

Challenge

Tammuz is the name of the ancient Babylonian sun god. The sun is the epitome of nature, of powerful forces that trick us into thinking that they have a power of their own. It was in Tammuz that we had our greatest fall as a nation. On the sixteenth day of Tammuz, the Jews eagerly awaited Moshe's return with the luchos. He did not come.

Some of the people, terrified of facing the desert without their leader, decided to fashion for themselves an icon of spiritual force. On the seventeenth of Tammuz, they created a golden calf. The egel was the force of idolatry — of man believing in himself rather than in Hashem. The tragedy of this misguided thinking echoed in other misfortunes occurring in the same month throughout the centuries.

But Tammuz is not a hopeless month. It is a month of challenge, a month when we have to put effort into seeing life as it really is and not as it appears.

As parents, we feel enormous responsibility toward our children, for their well-being, their happiness, and for the ultimate direction their lives take. We should always feel responsible, but never ultimately responsible. When we feel omniscient — claiming final credit for the good or even accepting absolute blame for the bad — we are falling into the "Tammuz trap." We are forgetting the Force that we don't see; the third Partner Who accompanies every couple in the task of childrearing. Bringing Him into our homes and lives is specifically the challenge of Tammuz, and, essentially, of every month.

Creampuff Moments

There are moments we wish would disappear from our memories, be swallowed up in our past, leaving no trace, no painful residue. Most of those moments involve our doing something we wish could be undone: harsh words we dream of stuffing back into our mouth, hasty actions we yearn to erase. But sometimes, our regret comes from our inertia, our inability to stand up for what was right while there was still time. That something right can be as trivial as a plate of creampuffs ....

Several years ago, when I was employed as a social worker, my boss asked me to arrange social events for the women our agency helped. Most of our clients were mothers of large families who were being crushed under the double burden of too much stress and too little money. Social ties were weak, and emotional resources were not often present. My boss dreamed of arranging monthly events which would give the women a much-needed social outlet as well as foster interdependence.

I had the necessary experience — I had co-headed our block's Neshei events for a number of years. Now I just had to trim the template I already used to make it fit a very different population. I picked themes, invited speakers, planned activities, and arranged for refreshments.

Much as none of us like to admit it, food is a very important component in any social event. Serve good food, and, providing the event itself isn't abysmal, people will leave feeling satisfied, physically and emotionally. When the food is mediocre, even the best speaker will often leave people grumbling. So I spent a considerable amount of time thinking about refreshments. I wanted the women to be active participants. I therefore made a general appeal to all the women invited to bring a nice milchig or parve dish.

This was a gamble; a number of these women had a difficult time getting their kids to school on time. Would they be able to find the time and energy to whip up quiches and cakes? The night before the brunch, I made a huge Greek salad and prayed it wouldn't be the only food present.

My prayers were answered. I walked into the community center the next morning and was greeted with groaning tables. There were homemade rolls, little hors d'oeuvres, a cornucopia of salads, and desserts with enough calories to knock any scale out of whack. The crowning glory was a big platter filled with homemade creampuffs. It was clear that an enormous amount of time and effort had gone into making these creampuffs. They were perfectly formed, filled with fluffy cream, and drizzled beautifully with chocolate.

I asked around to find out who was the creator of these delicate confections. Someone pointed out Avital, shy, withdrawn

Avital who seemed perpetually unsure of herself. I was surprised and thrilled — even if nothing else came of this event, Avital's showcasing her culinary skills to a large group of women would have justified its existence. I quickly went over to Avital to give her a warm compliment. She was standing a few feet away from her creampuffs, receiving a shower of praise. Her face had an uncharacteristic glow. My heart sang.

Tempting as the food looked, courtesy dictated that nobody touch it until after the speech by the well-known rebbetzin we had invited. I noticed the rebbetzin enter the room and tried to usher the women to the seats we'd arranged. But there was something else I was noticing, and it caused a worm of worry to eat at my heart.

As the room filled up with women, there were a surprising number of children as well. Not just small babies, as I'd expected, but three-, four-, and five-year-olds. The cacophony and din were growing by the moment, and I had to dodge a group of pre-schoolers playing tag. I'd clearly stated that this was for women only. What had happened?

Then it dawned on me. I'd set the date for Rosh Chodesh thinking it would be a nice time to have a get-together. What I hadn't taken into account is that on Rosh Chodesh, many preschools end early. Rather than have to leave the party early, many mothers had opted to pick up the kids and bring them along. I offered up another prayer, this one that all go well despite the many little people racing around the hall.

The rebbetzin began speaking. I listened with half an ear, while spending the rest of my time watching what was going on. The kids, bored of their game of tag, were headed over to the refreshment tables. There were bowls of pretzels and chips. I hoped mightily that they would limit their foraging to those snacks. For a while they did.

Then they began eyeing the more tempting morsels. Three of them stood before the creampuffs, whispering and pointing. From across the room I silently mouthed, "NO!" They didn't notice me. After a little more whispering, the most daring of the trio reached out and grabbed one of the exquisite treats. Her two friends followed suit. Once the dam broke, a flood ensued. One by one, each kid marched up to the table, grabbed a creampuff, and walked off, face buried in cream and chocolate. Not one mother protested.

I looked on in horror, torn with indecision. Should I get up during the lecture, walk across the room, and take away the plate? Cover it? Stand by and guard it? I was young and unused to being in a position of authority. I didn't want to make a scene. So I took the easy way out. I did nothing. I sat rooted to my chair, watching the miserable scene unfold. It took just six agonizing minutes for the entire plate to be emptied. Not one creampuff remained.

I looked over at Avital. Her shoulders were slumped, her eyes downcast. She had once again been given clear proof that it simply wasn't worthwhile trying — nothing works out the way you want. The hours she had spent had all vanished into the mouths of unappreciative tots, while not a single one of her friends so much as tasted a morsel.

As soon as I saw Avital, I realized the enormity of my mistake. Yes, I should have stood up. Yes, I should have stopped the children, and set down the much-needed boundaries that their parents were not providing. Yes, I should have preserved Avital's efforts and allowed her to receive the recognition she deserved and so desperately needed. But I hadn't. All that was left were sticky faces and a regret-laden heart.

I wish I could erase that creampuff moment from my mind forever, wipe the picture of the empty tray and Avital's slumped shoulders from my mental photo album. Yet every once in a while, at the slightest provocation, the image arises once again and my heart constricts in pain. But perhaps that's not a bad thing. For it serves as a regular reminder that doing nothing is an active choice; that neglecting to act can be just as deadly as doing the wrong thing.

As the Chinese proverb counsels, "Many a false step is made by standing still."

Charming Child
for Sale

I'm one of those gullible folk who actually reads the
back label on the products I buy, and even believe
a bit of the hype, at least until I try the product. I
love to hear about how the new model airplane I
bought my son will improve his hand-eye coordination, help him
learn persistence and patience, and give him a quality product
that he will cherish for years. I soak in the descriptions on the
back of the sterile, antiseptic face-cleansing pads telling me that
using them nightly will make my skin smooth, baby-soft, and free
of all pimples and blemishes. I relish the thought of the colorful
sprinkles I purchased adding pizzazz and class to my culinary
creations and setting my cakes a cut above the rest.

I conveniently forget that models often frustrate my son, he always needs my husband's help for the tricky parts, and the finished product never survives more than several weeks. It slips my mind that I tend to eat a tad too much chocolate, and the result is lodged in my facial pores. I fail to take into account that I will have to make the dazzling cake that my sprinkles are supposed to adorn.

Still, words have real power. Watching my son bend over the model, I congratulate myself over having chosen the toy that will help him develop patience. After swiping my face and feeling the satisfying tingle, I gaze into the mirror and can almost convince myself that the stubborn blackhead on my chin has been reduced in size. And when I pour a generous dose of sprinkles over the chocolate cake that never rose, the cake seems to be redeemed from its mediocrity.

I recently found myself thinking about how wonderful it would be if each child had his own personal advertising agent to help us discover his hidden treasures. Imagine if rambunctious Suri, who never manages to go a week without a visit to the principal, had been born with a glossy, neon pink tag. The tag would extol her verve and energy, her humor and pep, describe the way she lights up any room she enters, and adds zest to any project in which she takes part. If her harried mother could read that again and again, would it not help her focus on Suri's electric smile as opposed to the teacher's note?

Imagine if quiet Chaim — the Chaim who can't seem to make too many friends, and never says much — came along with pastel green wrapping and a promise of tranquility and peace. If his blurb spoke about an inner depth and a mature sensitivity to others and to the world around him, would it not help his father the next time he saw his son on the sidelines as his friends tossed a ball around?

Sounds unrealistic? It is. Can some sugar-coated sentences make a significant dent in the very real frustration and exasperation we sometimes feel when we come face to face with our children's shortcomings? No, I don't believe it can. But it could afford a second look, a glimpse of the power of the personality we are to help develop. Advertising is rarely blatant lying. There is usually a kernel of truth beneath the fluff. That kernel draws us, and entices us to believe that all the empty promises around it are also accurate. What we can do is find — and then not lose sight of — that inner kernel within each child.

So often our child's greatest strengths are the very traits which seem to be their undoing. The aspects that define who they are at the very core are the qualities that will both propel them and confound them throughout their lives. A good salesman knows how to flip any liability into an asset. The car isn't small; it's streamlined. The house isn't old; it's quaint and has character. Can we not do the same? Moishe isn't impulsive; he's quick and creative. Chani isn't bossy; she has leadership qualities. Doing this exercise a few times may yield surprising results. Lo and behold, there is truth in both descriptions. For the latter is simply a peek at the flip side of the former.

This all dawned on me tonight as I battled with my one-year-old son through our nightly routine. He screamed as I took him out of the bath, refused to let me put on his pajamas, howled as I tried to make supper. "What a difficult baby," was what my subconscious mind kept telling me. I caught myself. "What an independent little person," I replied, "unable to talk, yet able to express his feelings so eloquently."

Was he any different as a result? No, he was not.

But I was.

Getting Away

We planned our first family vacation this summer. We'd been to the States for family simchas, and gone away several times with my parents and siblings. But this was the first time it would be just us, on a real vacation, in cities my children have never seen. I was so excited

I managed to arrange an apartment swap with an acquaintance. I asked her for trip recommendations, tourist favorites, and bus schedules, and provided the same on my end. We wrote each other almost daily for weeks, planning every detail, getting the numbers of taxi drivers, pizza deliveries, and Shabbos takeout.

This was going to be a dream family vacation. During the past few weeks I had been very preoccupied and stressed, and had not had nearly enough patience for my kids. This was going to give me a chance to get away from everything and everyone, and focus exclusively on the lights of my life. It would be quality *and* quantity time. My children would discover our beautiful land and I'd be right beside them, rediscovering it through their eyes. We'd create memories that we'd carry in our hearts forever.

My husband and I had originally planned on telling the kids about our trip after Tisha B'av, less than a week before departure. That way, if our plans somehow fell through, they wouldn't be disappointed. But I couldn't contain myself. One Friday night, as we all sat around the table, I looked at each of them and then blurted out, "Guess what? We're all going to Tzefas this summer. Just us, for a whole week. It's going to be such fun."

The questions exploded around me. I answered and beamed. The kids soaked up all the plans I had, eager to take in every scrap of information I could give. But later that night, after they'd fallen asleep, I confided to my husband that I'd hoped for a bit more in their reaction — more exuberance, a little more anticipation. "Goodness, Bassi," he exclaimed, "they were bursting with excitement. They couldn't stop talking about it. What else could they have done?"

We got our answer the next day. We were eating the cholent when the kids informed us, stammering and blushing, that they had something to tell us. Then the three older ones lined up in front of the couch and broke into song.

"We're going to Tzefas. We're going to Tzefas. Tzefas is so much fun …."

They'd made up a song about our trip, complete with lyrics, motions, and an original tune that was an off-tune hybrid of two songs on a popular disk we'd just received. They sang it for us twice, my seven-year-old loudly prompting my five-year-old, who kept forgetting the verses. I listened, I watched, and I dabbed at my eyes. This was just as I'd dreamed.

The next two weeks came and went. I laundered more clothing than I thought we owned, and skimmed through a few more guidebooks. Finally, we had just one more day to go. I scrambled to get my last few articles written; I packed and repacked, washed even more laundry, and scrubbed my entire house so that the family coming would want to swap again. My husband and I had three hours of sleep that night.

In the morning, my husband bought fancy bottles of chocolate milk for the kids and iced coffee for us. He made nice sandwiches and packed loads of nosh. I threw in some last-minute essentials and laid out fresh linen and towels. Then we lugged out all the luggage, my husband muttering something about the kitchen sink.

The driver who was supposed to take us to Yerushalayim, where we were meant to catch our bus to Tzefas, was late. My stomach clenched. The busses only ran every two hours. We called him. He'd be there in five minutes, he told us. They were five very long minutes. He finally came, and we set off.

We reached Yerushalayim in record time, and I began breathing again. We pulled up to the spot where our neighbor had said there would be a Tzefas bus stop. But there was no bus stop to be found. We cruised around a bit, the minute hand of my watch sweeping around at a frightening pace. We spotted a bus stop that looked right. But the taxi couldn't reach it — it was in a bus-only lane. The driver dropped us off nearby, dumping our luggage on the sidewalk. My husband went off to double-check. It wasn't the right stop. The driver was gone. We had less than fifteen minutes until the bus would pull up to the impossible-to-find stop.

The kids were wailing that they were hungry. We'd forgotten to wash. I found a falafel shop, asked permission to use the sink, and shepherded all the kids inside. I found the sandwiches and gave each kid a bite. My husband raced up and down the long street, trying to find the bus stop. Finally he came back, triumphant. He'd found it. We all grabbed a piece of luggage and set out. We were nearly there when an awful realization hit me. The stop was on the wrong side of the street. It was for the bus coming *from* Tzefas, not going *to* it. We had five minutes to go. The baby was wailing to be fed. Why, oh why, had I ever decided to do this???!!

We made it in the end, reaching the correct stop moments before the bus pulled up. We piled on and sank into our seats. And then the fighting for the window seat began. And then the bickering over the bigger brownie commenced. And then the wailing over who had kicked the back of whose seat started. And then, an hour-and-a-half away from Tzefas, the bus broke down. We sat in a sweltering bus station for half-an-hour, finishing all our snacks, before we were sent onto a new bus. Someone took the seats we had been in on the first bus so we ended up with four seats for seven people. And then, as it chugged up the hill to Tzefas, the bus broke down again.

Seven hours after we'd left our home, we reached Tzefas. Only to discover that the home that would be ours for the next week was perched atop one of the steepest hills we had ever seen. And it had no air conditioning.

Somehow we managed to unpack, do a huge shopping to stock the house with food, take the kids out for falafel, and make plans for the next day. "Just six more days," I whispered to my husband as we finally collapsed into bed. The term "family vacation," I'd realized, was the biggest oxymoron out there.

Things looked a bit better after a few hours of sleep and some breakfast. That first day we went to a big, beautiful park in a quiet wooded area. We brought along a disposable grill and a fabulous lunch. I started feeling hopeful. But, amazingly, the children still bickered. About who would get the first hotdog. About who would get the best swing. About who would sit next to the window in the cab home. And, equally amazing, I got just as annoyed as I normally did. I cajoled, threatened, and snapped. What had happened to all the bonding we were supposed to be doing? What had happened to the tender memories we were meant to be creating?

It was on the last night of our trip that the brutal truth hit me. No matter where we went, no matter what we did, we would essentially remain the same people. My baby wouldn't decide to forego her feedings simply because we were in a crowded public area. My kids wouldn't have a personality overhaul simply because we had traveled halfway across the country. I wouldn't become a serene, ever-patient mother simply because I had left my computer at home. Real change requires a lot more than a digital camera and a cooler. I could get away from my home and my job; but I could never get away from myself. So I'd best try to spend the rest of the year becoming the type of person I'd like to vacation with. Just 358 more days to go ....

Hidden — Not Lost

*L*ast week I had a date with one of my favorite people. My nine-year-old son and I spent an evening together in Geula, a major shopping district in Yerushalayim. The idea germinated in my mind after a particularly stressful afternoon. Lately, my relationship with my eldest is not what I'd like it to be. Power struggles, belligerence, and defiance seem normal. It became worrisome when that seemed to be the standard fare for the two of us. I realized I was probably overdrawn in my love account with him and decided to make a big deposit.

I met him after school and we took the bus into town. On the bus he marveled at the new checkpoint they are building on the border of the Green Line and asked me numerous questions about how terrorists get into the country, how they construct their bombs, and a variety of other gory topics. Keeping my breathing steady, I answered him as briefly as I could, and then changed the subject. We talked about the contests he's having at school and his friend's new collection. He thrust himself in front of the mirror over the back door and made funny faces — and I said nothing

When we reached Yerushalayim, we did errands together. Everywhere we went, I tried to get something nice for him. In the clothing store, we picked out two new flannel shirts. In the bookstore, he used his Chanukah gelt to purchase two biographies of gedolim. He has thirteen such books at home, none of which he's managed to read; but I said nothing. At the nut store, I bought him a small bag of popcorn, and at the stationery store, we picked out an inexpensive toy.

Finally, with full bags and empty stomachs, we headed for one of the many greasy fleishig restaurants that dot the area like freckles. Eyes big, standing ten-feet tall, my son ordered a jumbo piece of schnitzel, a slice of Yerushalmi kugel, and a portion of spaghetti with sauce. I mentally calculated the carbohydrate and fat content of that meal — and said nothing. When he picked up his ketchup-smeared schnitzel and ate it with his hands — I said nothing. We sat across from each other, and schmoozed while we ate. It was gratifyingly pleasant to converse with him. During the bus ride home, we sat in drowsy, companionable silence.

"Are you tired?" I asked.

"No, I'm happy," he replied. And despite my aching legs and pounding head, I was so glad I had carved out this time for the two of us.

The next day, as he bounded in after cheder I greeted him enthusiastically. He brushed off my greeting and demanded food, claiming he was starving. I gave him several options. He didn't like any of them. His sister annoyed him just then, and he responded inappropriately. And suddenly, we were back to the bad place I had dreamed of leaving. I was screaming, and so was he. The power struggle was on. I tried to take a step back, to salvage what we had obtained the day before, but it was slipping out of my grasp like water at the seashore.

By the end of the evening, I felt utterly deflated. We had had a horrible day, my boy and I. The glow of the previous night had been replaced by a smoldering fire. Had it all been in vain? Were the good times lost forever?

The next day was Friday, short and stressful. With four guests for Shabbos and a minor work crisis to deal with, I didn't have a spare minute. So I was considerably discombobulated to realize that Menucha's glasses were not on her nose — nor in their case. Nor were they on top of the toilet in the bathroom, not were they next to her art project on the dining-room table, nor were they tucked away in her bed. I felt panic rising. Those glasses are only six-months-old. They cost nearly $100. Where were they?

My husband remained calm. "Remember when the lens fell out of her glasses and we rushed to replace it, and then it showed up three days later?" Boy, did I remember. "They didn't walk off. Just relax — we'll find them." But the longer we looked, the more likely it seemed that they had sprouted a pair of legs. We moved furniture, overturned drawers, rummaged through stacks of papers — and came up empty-handed. I was mentally fitting a visit to the optician into my Sunday schedule and trying to squeeze this unwanted expense into our monthly budget.

As a last-ditch effort, my husband gathered all the kids and waved a bag of treats in front of them. "Anyone who looks for the glasses gets a multi-colored sour stick," he announced, "and whoever finds them, gets this," and he dangled a swizzle lolly and sugar packet before their eyes. Sufficiently motivated, they fanned out and checked every place we had looked, and then some. The glasses were not to be found.

Ten minutes before candle lighting, my husband had a flash of inspiration. He instructed my daughter to check her backpack. And there, nestled between notebooks and a pencil case, were her blue-rimmed glasses. They'd never looked so nice. The knot in my stomach untied, and I leapt into the shower.

———•◦•———

Hours later, I thought about the wisdom of my husband's attitude. The glasses weren't gone forever; they were just temporarily hidden. I could have saved myself an inordinate amount of stress by just letting the situation ride — by doing what I could to find them, without moaning about the worst-possible scenario.

And I wondered about the other item I seemed to have lost in the past week. Is my golden evening with my son truly obliterated, or is it just temporarily hidden? Would it not be wisest to just let the relationship ride the waves — by doing what I can to remedy it, without resigning myself to the worst possible scenario? For might I not find the results of our positive interactions in the most unexpected of places and times — if only I allow them to appear?

Among the Blessed

As the spring breezes and budding bushes of April and May change to the sultry heat of June, it becomes clear that summer has arrived. The beginning of summer heralds the end of the school year. Most students simply dream of casting aside books and pens and plunging into pools. But some have a milestone to cross in between the two. Graduation is a poignant mix of hope for the future and memories of the past. Anticipation of a new chapter in life mingles with tendrils of fear of leaving the familiar. For parents of the graduates, graduating signifies yet another giant step their child is taking upon the path to adulthood.

While I've a number of years ahead of me before I will watch my child in cap and gown march across a stage to accept a rolled and beribboned diploma, I've been to a fair share of mini-graduations — those ubiquitous little end-of-the-year parties that every kindergarten teacher feels it is her sacred duty to hold. The children practice for weeks, bring home brightly-colored invitations, and invite Bubby as well. On the big day, they dress in white shirts and blue pants and skirts — the classic Israeli outfit for important occasions — and sing their hearts out. They sing about becoming big, about learning and growing; they sing thanks to their teachers and mothers. Half the words are beyond their vocabulary, but that doesn't prevent them from belting them out with childish enthusiasm.

With nursery and kindergarten stretched out over four years here in Israel, and several children close in age, every June finds me shifting uncomfortably in a hard plastic seat as I listen to one of my offspring serenade me and exult in her passage to the future.

And every year, as they sing the words about their Ima, the touching rhymes thanking mothers for all they are and do, I cry. As I rummage through my purse for a tissue, I think of another woman — one I've never met, but with whom I feel a genuine connection.

————————

I was young when I read the book, just out of my teens. I had only recently started the shidduch scene, and dreamed of a rosy future surrounded by a devoted husband and cherubic children. A friend lent me the slender volume when I complained of nothing to read. It was the story of one woman's journey through infertility. With searing honesty, the author chronicles her trials and tests, her disappointments and near despair. It takes years and much heartache, but she is finally blessed with two children. Their births leave her ill, but that doesn't diminish the overwhelmingly powerful love she has for the souls she has managed to bring into this world.

One of the very last pages of the book describes the kindergarten graduation of her oldest child, her personal miracle. She writes of the other mothers yawning, looking at their watches, snapping a few dutiful pictures while they mentally compose shopping lists for the grocery. She, on the other hand, is engulfed with emotion. She is sitting with other mothers, watching her child as he leaves kindergarten forever. She has emerged from a tunnel of darkness. She is among the blessed. When her little boy sings a *thank you* to Ima, she unabashedly weeps with joy.

Although I had yet to find my husband, much less have children, I was deeply struck by this scene. Why, I couldn't help but wonder, does a woman have to struggle with years of infertility to be able to truly appreciate a milestone in her child's life? Must we first be denied a gift in order to feel gratitude upon receiving it? With the righteous indignation of the young, I found myself angry at the other mothers at the graduation. Simply because the blessings had flowed down upon them naturally, did they not realize how blessed they were?

Years passed. I married, and just several weeks after our first anniversary, our first son was born. The next child was not long in coming. Infertility was not among my personal tests; my challenge was keeping my head above water as I awoke three times a night and changed more diapers than I could count. The days seemed endless, but the months flew by, and before I knew it, I was sitting at a second kindergarten graduation. I watched for a while, took a few pictures, held back a yawn, and sneaked a look at my watch.

It was then that I remembered her. I thought of the scene — of the previously barren woman rejoicing in her child, awash in euphoria over meriting to sit at a kindergarten graduation. I wrested my eyes away from my wrist. I focused fully and unreservedly upon my daughter. I gazed at her delicate features, took note of her effervescence, reveled in her exuberance. And when she reached the song about Ima, I wept. I am a mother, and I too have my own little miracles. Thanks to the One above, I am among the blessed.

Destruction

Av is a month of tragedy and loss. It is the month during which both Batei Mikdash were destroyed, the month in which the Jews were expelled from Spain, and the month during which World War I, the precursor to World War II, broke out. It is the month in which our very existence was threatened, as nation after nation tried to destroy G-d's chosen people. Yet, we emerged from every disaster that assailed us, revived and rebuilt.

Hashem promised us that we would never disappear as a nation. That promise had two aspects. If we tried to disappear — to become one with the culture that hosted us — that culture would turn upon us, treating us with such horrific cruelty that it would become abundantly clear that we could never join them.

But the destruction brought upon us, however awful, would never be total. We would rise up from the ashes and begin anew. It is on Tishah B'Av, the darkest day in the Jewish calendar, that Mashiach will be born. That is the second aspect of Hashem's promise; redemption will always follow destruction, the pain of labor is followed by birth.

The metaphor of birth is particularly powerful for mothers. We can easily relate to the difficulty and the ecstasy of birth. But we are often less aware of the smaller microcosms of this process that can be found within each day. The labor of sealing our lips can give birth to the beauty of connection. The labor of expending extra effort — effort we are sure we cannot muster — can foster appreciation and love. The labor of rising above our own nature, transcending hurt feelings and bruised egos, can give birth to children able to do the same.

The cause and effect are not immediate. At times, all we see is unappreciated effort, unrequited devotion. But just as the destruction of Av stems from the same source that fuels the approaching Redemption, so too our efforts are not for naught. Our labor will bear us bountiful fruit.

Bring Us Back

Yerushalayim, 3830 (70 CE)

T he flames leapt higher and higher, tongues of red licking the very heavens. Elisheva stood rooted to the ground, unable to remove her eyes from the ghastly sight of the core of her existence being destroyed. The Beis HaMikdash was burning. She felt as though it were her soul that was on fire.

There would be no more *korbanos*, no powerful physical connection between man and his Maker. There would be no more miracles shown openly, daily, for all to see. There would no more throngs of thousands gathered in the courtyard during the three *regalim*, all eager "to see and be seen," to receive the spiritual uplift that would carry them through the upcoming months. There would be no more revelation, no more clarity, no more direct contact with the One Above. No more. No more. No more.

Elisheva couldn't bear to watch the scene. Clutching her tiny son, she ran through the cobblestone streets of her beloved city. She ran and ran, trying desperately to get away from the pain.

But there was no escaping the utter destruction of her nation. Her path was blocked by corpses, the latest victims of the unrelenting famine that left one empty of all desire, save the aching need for a piece of bread. The streets flowed red with the blood of her slain brethren.

She couldn't return home — the empty rooms seemed to mock her, reminding her of the large, warm family that had once dwelled within those walls. They were all gone now, victims of the plague that had recently swept the city. Her mother and father, her husband and children, all gone. Only her infant remained.

She knew she wouldn't be in Yerushalayim much longer. The Roman captors had made it very clear that all those who had succeeded in escaping with their lives would not retain their freedom. This was her last day in the only city she had ever known.

Even as she ran, the heat chased her, stalked her steps, never allowing her to forget for even a moment that the Beis HaMikdash was being consumed by a raging fire. The holy vessels had all been taken to Rome by the evil ones. And now, the building that had been the focal point of the nation for over 400 years would be no more.

But she knew, deep down, that it had been consumed long ago. This fire was just the physical manifestation of the spiritual destruction that the Jewish nation had wrought. Their hatred of each other, the bad-mouthing, the backstabbing, the inability to accept people who were different — all that had slowly destroyed the Beis HaMikdash until only the shell remained. And now they had lost the shell as well.

In her arms, the baby stirred. She searched for a place where she could feed him. Finding an abandoned shack, she entered and settled down with her son. There was little she could give him — she herself hadn't eaten in days. He tried to fill his stomach, and his whimpers turned to howls when he was unsuccessful. Her tears joined his.

This little boy — he'd never know. He'd never know what could have, should have, been his. He'd never experience the tangible presence of Hashem. He'd never witness the overwhelming joy of the *simchas beis hashoeva*. He'd never know the elevation of bringing a *korban* for a misdeed – and knowing that the breach had been repaired.

He'd grow up in Rome, far from all she held dear. And he wouldn't even know what he had lost.

"Bring him back to You," she whispered fiercely over her baby's cries. "Bring him back. And with him, all of us."

Poland, 5683 (1923)

"Put down that book, Mira, and don't you ever read it again. My daughter will not defile her mind with secular novels written by atheists."

Mira put down the book, but the defiant toss of curls as she did so let Faigy know that the defeat was temporary — Mira would finish that book, and others as well. Mira did what she wanted.

Faigy bit her lip and turned away. When had it started? Girls had been attending the secular gymnasiums in Poland for years. But they had always know that it was an unavoidable evil, one to be endured and then forgotten as quickly as possible as one immersed oneself in the important goals of life. When had it become something more? When had the girls begun relishing their secular studies, taking them further and further? When had the schools captured their hearts as well as their minds?

Mira was one of the victims, pulled into the empty ideologies her teachers espoused in school. She looked to *them*, not to the Torah, for her direction in life. Faigy was losing her daughter.

Faigy thought back to the other daughter she had lost. Little Miriam had been only four weeks old when a pogrom had started in their small village. Mother and daughter had both been attacked. Faigy had recovered from her wounds. Miriam had not.

But even that agony had been better than what she was enduring now. She could live with a child whose body was gone. She could not live with one who was losing her soul.

The next time she saw the book was at the Shabbos table. They had been sitting around the table, Mottel and the boys sharing pearls of Torah, she listening with joy. Then Mottel told Mira to help serve the soup, and as Mira rose from her place, the accursed novel had fallen to the floor. Mottel had risen in a rage. "Get out," he had yelled in a voice contorted with fury. "Take that terrible book and leave."

Mira snatched the book and ran from the room, from the house. She disappeared into the inky blackness outside.

Faigy stayed up all night saying *tehillim* as tears rolled down her cheek. But Mira hadn't returned.

It was only on Sunday morning that a neighbor informed Faigy that Mira had joined the socialist youth group.

She would not be coming home.

Faigy cried all the time now. She cried as she cooked and cleaned. She cried when she davened and when she lit candles. Her tears and her prayers were all she had left.

"Bring her back to You," she would beg, "bring her back. And with her, all of us."

She knocked timidly on the door. "Yanky. Yanky, it's very late; the last minyan is already starting. You have to get up and go to daven." Faigy hoped her voice wouldn't betray the desperation that she felt.

"Go away," a voice growled from within. "Just leave me alone, won't you? And how many times do I have to tell you — it's Jack, not Yanky."

Two minutes later she could hear her son's snores.

Faigy walked away with slumped shoulders. She didn't know why she bothered. Minyan was the least of Yanky's problems. She wasn't even sure he kept Shabbos any more. A number of the kids in that new group he had started hanging out with openly smoked on Shabbos. And she was pretty certain that it wasn't just cigarettes that they were smoking.

Images arose in Faigy's mind. She saw her son at his Chumash party, celebrating the day he had begun to learn Chumash. His curly *peyos* bounced beneath his crown; his face beamed with a light that seemed to come from his very *neshamah*.

But by the time he celebrated his first siyum, the smile had dimmed somewhat. Yanky had trouble reading, trouble understanding, trouble keeping up. How they had tried — she and Moish both learned with him, and they hired the best tutors. But he continued to struggle.

By the time he began Mishnayos, her little boy was closed as tight as a hibiscus at night, secretive and mysterious in all he did.

By the time his class began Gemara, Yanky was no longer amongst them.

Faigy walked back to the steamy kitchen. The heat she felt was not just from the rising temperatures outside. It came from within. It was the heat of the flames that had burned long ago.

The heat of the destruction of that which had connected man and his Creator. The searing heat of the pain of separation.

She put up eggs to boil for the *seudah hamafsekes* they would eat that night. Her tears began to flow freely into the pot.

"Bring him back to You," she pleaded, "bring him back. And with him, all of us."

Of Fares and Fairness

$\mathcal{I}$f my husband hadn't been at my side, I never would have ventured into the cab. With his metal-studded leather jacket, spiked hair, and silver earring, the driver wasn't the type to inspire a feeling of safety and security. But my husband had no qualms, so we slid into the back seat.

We were on a vacation in Netanya for several days. My parents had invited our family of four to join them on their summer holiday. We were all staying in a converted school dormitory that was a convenient and affordable resort. During the day we had taken a jolly family trip. After we had bathed the kids and bedded them down, my mother offered to keep an eye on them while we went out together. We'd had a lovely evening relishing our privacy, and now we had to head back. It was late at night, but we managed to hail a cab with ease.

"Hi," the driver said in a genuinely friendly voice. "Where to?"

We named the school-turned-vacation-resort at which we were staying, and he started driving. I glanced at the meter. It was off. I felt my adrenaline rush. This is one of the nastier tricks that some Israeli cab drivers like to play. They don't turn on the meter and then charge you whatever they please when you reach your destination. But I wasn't a greenhorn; I'd lived here for years and I wasn't going to fall for that one.

"The meter, please," I said in even tones.

"You're from another city, aren't you?" the cabbie replied.

"Yes," I answered, rather puzzled, "and I'd really like to drive with the meter."

"Trust me," he said, "it's not worth it for you."

Sure, the cynic within me said, *I'm going to trust you. Why on earth would I do that?* But he went on to explain. "Here in Netanya, we have a different system. There's a set price for every destination. It costs ten shekel in the city center, fifteen for the outskirts, and so on. It's thirty-five shekel for the school you need."

The price sounded right but I'd been burned too many times. I was still leery. "Maybe we'll just take the meter anyway," I said.

The fellow shrugged. "Listen, lady," he finally said, "I'll put on the meter, but I'm not going to charge you according to the amount it says. I just want to show you how badly you'd be ripped off if you'd do it that way."

I was mollified, and finally allowed myself to sit back and breathe.

After a moment he resumed talking. "Many cabbies would have jumped at your suggestion. They live off of strangers who don't know the system here. But I wouldn't do that. There's a G-d in the world. He knows the system and I know that I'm not allowed to cheat. In any case, G-d decided at the beginning of the year how much money I was going to earn. I won't earn a penny more than that, so why would I be dishonest?"

I listened in thoughtful silence. What struck me was not just his firm conviction, but the fact that he lived his life based upon those principles. Many of us believe that Hashem sets the amount we are meant to earn, and no amount of dishonesty will earn us a penny more. But how many of us live our lives acting upon this belief? We allow Hashem into our shuls and kitchens but somehow leave Him behind when we have to pull out our wallets. This man — spiked hair, metal jewelry, and all — was actually living what we were supposed to believe. He certainly seemed like a strange teacher. But this was Eretz Yisrael and I'd long ago learned that what you see if often not what you get.

We continued driving in silence. Finally, we pulled up to the driveway of the school. He switched off the meter. "Fifty-four shekel," he said triumphantly. "You would have had to pay me almost twenty shekel more if we would have done it your way."

He turned around and gave us a brilliant smile. It glowed far brighter than the earring in his ear.

Soldier's Mother

Shivah Assar B'Tamuz. The kids are home early from camp. They are very bored. We're playing a game of Memory with cards depicting animals. My good friend calls. We chat for several minutes, and then she drops the bombshell.

"You know, I assume, that our country is at war."

I'm looking for the other goose. I know I've seen it somewhere. As I scan the cards before me, her words don't seem to register. "War?" I echo dumbly. I flip a card. Wrong — it's the goat. My daughter gleefully picks the two geese and places the set on her ever-growing pile.

"Yes," my friend replies. "Hezbollah captured two soldiers and killed eight. They are firing rockets into northern Israel. The IDF is retaliating. It doesn't look good."

My stomach knots. She can't tell me much more; it's too early to tell where this will lead. I hang up. I finish the Memory game. I make lunch for the kids. Then, I check the news. I shudder at the horror of it all, and pray for the safety of all those in danger.

Ever since, I feel as if I'm leading a double life. On the surface, there is nary a ripple in the calm lake of my life. I play with, bathe, clothe, and feed my children. They set off happily for camp each morning, and return bursting with tales of their exciting day. The shopping, cooking, and laundry all get done.

When I get the occasional frantic email from a concerned friend abroad, I feel a deep guilt. My daily routine is no different than it was a month ago. At least not on the surface. Inside, waves of emotion crash upon the shore, sometimes engulfing it, and then the tears flow.

It's the pictures that hit me the hardest. Looking closely at the faces of the soldiers involved in deadly missions, I'm perpetually shocked by how young they are. Boys — really, the same age as my kid brother — are setting out for battle in tanks that can, and do, become fiery graves. In one photo, they are advancing on foot toward a house suspected of harboring terrorists. I feel a deep dread as I wonder what greeted those soldiers as they burst through the door. Are all of them still with us?

The image that returns to haunt me is one of a mortally-wounded soldier being evacuated after the deadly fighting for Bint Jbeil. There's an oxygen mask over the wounded boy's face. It's the face of his companion, who is wheeling him back home, that I cannot forget. His features are contorted in agony. As he helplessly watches his friend slip away, pain and horror radiate from his eyes. I can't bear to think of how the fallen-soldier's mother must have looked, when the army officers knocked on her door and told her that her son would never come home.

As a mother myself, it is the mothers of the men risking their lives to protect me who are in the forefront of my mind. I chirp a cheery goodbye to my son as he heads off to cheder, and I think of her, the nameless, faceless entity I've labeled "soldier's mother." When did she last say goodbye to her son? Was it before the region exploded in craziness? Did she know the danger ahead? Perhaps she simply pecked him lightly on the cheek, pressing homemade goodies into his hands, as he headed off to his base. Or maybe they saw each other more recently. Maybe, knowing where he was headed, she leaned down to whisper how deeply she loves him. In either case, the image of that goodbye must loom large in her mind. She knows that it may be goodbye forever.

I think of her when my phone rings. I get it if I can. I leave it if I can't. Not she. She sits beside that phone all day, hoping and waiting. Waiting for her son to let her know, "Don't worry, Mom, I'm still alive." When the call finally comes, she breathes a sigh of relief. And then waits for the next call.

When I slide into bed at the end of an exhausting day and allow myself to drift off into a deep sleep, she rises into my consciousness. Her sheets are twisted and her heart constricted, as she lies in the silence, trying not to think of where her little boy may be at that very moment.

I think of her when there's a knock on the door. I answer it calmly. My heart doesn't race nor my pulse quicken. I know that behind that door will stand a neighbor or an indigent fellow collecting tzedakah. I have no fear of facing a group of three army officials bearing shattering news.

And when my kids are particularly cute and I get that expansion of joy inside my heart — I think of soldier's mother then, too. I think of how her son must have been this cute as well. And pray that he come home safe, so one day his children will be giving her that same happiness.

After the War

The war is over, the guns silenced. Israel is mourning her dead, caring for her wounded, and trying to convince her people, and the rest of the world, that this battle was not in vain. I know too little about politics to appreciate the shifts that occurred in Israel's military and political standing as a result of the thirty-four days of mayhem. I can only know the little changes that occurred within; the ways in which I view the world differently, now that the bloody battles in Lebanon are no more.

———•••———

I've been living in this tiny land well over a dozen years. There are many things I love, but some aspects that I find disturbing. One issue that has always earned my ire is the manner in which customers are treated. After having been accustomed to the VIP service that is offered to anyone who strolls into an American shop, it is rather disconcerting to be exposed to the Israeli attitude. As far as the Israeli storekeeper is concerned, it is *he* who is doing *you* a tremendous favor by giving you a chance to buy his products, not the other way around. The picture is scratched, the hem is ripped; well then, for heavens sake, don't buy it! Why should I offer it to you at a discounted price? You already paid for it, and then discovered the defect? These things happen, it should be a *kapparah*. Again and again, I'd find myself confused and exasperated by this attitude.

It was when I was reading an article about a wounded soldier that I was suddenly able to sympathize with their viewpoint. The soldier had no legs; he had lost them both in battle. He was a rock star, this young boy, and he strummed his guitar as he sat in his hospital bed. I didn't admire his choice of a profession, but I certainly admired his spirit. "If the loss of my legs will help bring Israel peace," he claimed, "then it was a worthwhile loss."

His parents stood off to the side in the picture shown. A middle-aged, non-religious couple, she with bleached-blond hair and he in a T-shirt and shorts, they wore an inscrutable expression as they looked at their crippled son. But their feelings they shared. "We received a gift — our son's life."

Many thoughts raced through my mind as I read those words: thoughts of wonder and admiration, thoughts of awe at their ability to perceive the world as a good place, to see not two missing legs, but a body and soul that are still intact. And beneath all that, was the honest realization. *Of course your typical Israeli can't be bothered with a tiny nick on my new cell phone. They know life is too short for that.*

This summer, we spent a week in Yerushalayim. My parents were away, and we moved in with my teen siblings. They watched my kids, I kept an eye on them, and everyone was happy. We invited a displaced family from the north to stay in our home while we were gone.

The father of the brood of eight came early to see the apartment and get the key. He was a gentle, soft-spoken fellow. What struck me was his equanimity. There was no hysteria over having to leave all that he owns upon this earth; no panic over the thought that his home may no longer exist by the time he returns. He wasn't angry at G-d, or anyone else, for that matter. There was a quiet acceptance of our enemies' hatred, and a steely resolve to retain his dignity. When he heard that we had precisely the number of beds that he needed, he was openly moved, and loudly blessed Hashem. His family took excellent care of the apartment, and left it even cleaner than they had received it.

———•◦•———

When I was a single girl, Motza'ei Shabbos was synonymous with trips to the Kosel. I appreciated the stillness of the ancient Wall at night; I relished starting my week by pouring out my heart at the holiest spot on earth; I appreciated joining the throngs of people who chose to do the same.

I've moved away from Yerushalayim, and I get to the Kosel far less frequently than I'd like. Finding myself in the sacred city for the week, I felt compelled to make my way to the Wall as Shabbos drew to a close. My husband and I put the kids to bed and slipped out.

The Kosel was as it has always been, brooding and silent, bathed in silver moonlight and endless tears. I found a spot and started davening. I was in middle of davening when they came: A big group, the women standing beside me, the men just a foot away on the other side of the mechitzah; it was clear they were here on a mission. Immediately, they began reciting chapter after chapter of *tehillim*, the men aloud and the women silently along with them. These were no ordinary prayers; these people were begging, pleading with Hashem for salvation. Sobbing punctuated their words as they poured out their hearts.

Standing beside them, I felt swept up in their pain. A family member must be deathly ill, I presumed. They must be beseeching Hashem for his very life. Apparently, I wasn't the only one who had come to that conclusion. I soon heard another woman asking one of the members of the group, "Who is it you're praying for? What is his name?"

The second woman was astonished. "Who is it for?" she echoed. "It's for all of Klal Yisrael. It's for the situation we are in now. That's what it's for."

I completed my *Shemonah Esrei* and joined them in their fervent prayers. It was hard to leave.

The war is over, the guns are silent. Many complain that nothing has changed. But I know that's not accurate — the people have.

A Full Empty Nest

I'm sure the Fines have completely forgotten about me. They would no doubt be surprised to discover how often I think of them. After all, our relationship was brief and fleeting — my family and I slept in their home one Shabbos, and then we parted ways. That visit, though, gave me a vision which has become my personal dream.

We met the Fines four years ago, when we spent Shabbos in New York. My brother had just gotten married to a wonderful girl from Boro Park, and the whole crew converged upon the neighborhood to be able to attend Shabbos sheva brachos. Not many people were eager to put up a couple with three young children, one of whom was a colicky seven-week-old baby. The Fines found it just fine. "We have several empty bedrooms that you are more than welcome to use. We'll probably sleep right through the baby's cries. And if we do hear her, well, it will be nice to have a baby in the house again."

We arrived at the Fine home several hours before Shabbos. The décor was Spartan. The rug was well-worn, the furniture simple — no ornate lamps or art-deco coffee tables here. The main decorations upon the walls and every available surface were pictures. Beautiful brides stood beside youthful grooms in a seemingly unending parade of wedding portraits. Toothless babies and impish toddlers smiled beside baby blocks, watering cans, and other Sears' photography props.

In short order, we discovered that the Fines had twelve children, all of whom were married, and an undisclosed number of grandchildren. We played "Jewish Geography" for a while. I didn't know their daughter in Yerushalayim, but her neighbor was my good friend. And my second cousin lived in the same small town where their fourth son had chosen to live.

I liked Mrs. Fine immediately. She was a straightforward, kind woman in her early sixties who said what she meant and meant what she said. Her husband was a quieter male version of those same traits. My children were making themselves at home — a situation which would normally cause me a fair amount of stress when staying with strangers. Here, though, our hosts seemed to genuinely enjoy our children's exuberance.

It was Friday, and we all had much to do. After our initial conversation, we went upstairs to unpack. The Fines bustled around finishing last-minute preparations for Shabbos. We both lit candles — she lit two ornate seven-branched candelabras, and I, five tea lights. Then, I hurried over to my new sister-in-law's home to join the festivities.

We were halfway through the meal before I realized that I had forgotten diapers for the baby. My toddler was cranky and needed a bed. Taking advantage of the *eiruv* the neighbors had constructed around their homes, I scooped up my toddler and set off for the Fines.

I knocked lightly and let myself in, as instructed. The first thing I heard was singing. The Fines were singing *zemiros* together, her soprano beautifully complimenting his ringing baritone. Their singing was like their personalities — simple yet rich. They engaged in no fancy harmonies, no trills or embellishments. But you could tell they were thinking about the words they were singing.

On my way to the steps, I had a clear view of their Shabbos table in the dining room. The two were sitting near each other, empty china soup bowls in front of them. At the end of the table, fourteen candles flickered. On the wall beside them was a photo taken three years earlier, at the wedding of their youngest child. It was a portrait of the children with their spouses — twenty-four people surrounding the Fines. It looked like a small army.

I lingered at the foot of the stairs. It was the atmosphere more than the scene itself which struck me. Even now, I grope for the words with which to describe the peace, the fulfillment, the contentment the Fines exuded.

"Empty nest" has always struck me as such a sad term. Once the nest was full of babies, alive with action. Now it's a hollow shell, devoid of the spark it once contained. I've had many a harried moment when I've dreamed of the day when my children will be grown, married, and in homes of their own, while I enjoy blessed, uninterrupted peace. Despite that, a finger of fear strikes my heart when I hear someone talk of an empty nest. Will the second half of my married life be spent listening to the echoes of what once was?

The Fines allowed me to glimpse an empty nest that was full. Filled with the couple's mutual respect and admiration. Filled with the sense of satisfaction which comes from raising a dozen children and watching them all put down roots of their own. Filled with pleasant memories which sustain rather than mock. On that Friday night, holding my toddler, fetching diapers for my infant, surrounded by my fledgling birds, I got a vision of how I want my nest to look when it is no longer filled with little ones.

That vision is not simply an amorphous image in the back of my mind, patiently waiting out the decades. Just as obvious as the Fines' contentment was the fact that such a state does not simply arrive as the last child steps out the front door. It is the accumulation of years and years of creating a good marriage, of keeping one's priorities intact, of building the type of home in which one would wish to spend the remainder of her days. That vision is a prompt, a reminder, a call to action. It prompts me to keep abreast of my husband's life and inner world, reminds me to carve out time for the two of us in the midst of the bustle of life with little people; it calls me to raise my children with respect, so we part in love and not in anger.

That vision has become a personal dream. No longer do I fear an empty nest. I think of a simple home in Boro Park, and I dream of contentment, of unity, and of flickering flames, one for each of the lights I have set upon this earth.

Stranger on the Hospital Stairs

I f I live one thousand years, I don't think I will ever forget that scene.

It was a balmy Shabbos morning. My grandmother was in the hospital, recovering from surgery. Young and single, I was able to make the three-quarter-hour walk to visit her, so she would have some company on Shabbos. My cousin, who was staying with us at the time, decided to come along. She wanted to visit her dorm mother who was in the same hospital, having given birth the day before. We walked together, enjoying the companionship and the spring sun.

We entered the dim lobby of the hospital, but even the somber mood we encountered there didn't douse our high spirits. I walked up to my grandmother's ward and promised my cousin I'd come pick her up. My grandmother was feeling relatively well, and our time together flew by. Soon enough, I was hiking up the stairs to the maternity ward.

He was seated on the stairs just outside the entrance to the ward. A young Yerushalmi chassid, dressed in a regal gold-and-white caftan, white socks tucked into black knickers — he was someone whose path I would normally never cross. Here, in this building of life and death, he was hunched over, head between such knees, sobbing with an intensity of agony I had never before witnessed. It came from the depths of his being, the cry of a misery that was too great to bear. It was a sound so laden with pain that I felt my insides tearing.

There was someone with him, a young teenager, probably a brother. His companion sat beside him, silent in the face of such grief. He showed his compassion with a hand laid across the other's shoulder. Yet it was clear there was little that he, or anyone else, could do.

I stood there on the stairwell, unwilling to trespass into the pain of a stranger. What, I thought, could have happened that would cause someone such grief in this one island of happiness in the hospital? Had he lost a baby, the dreams of nine months crushed in a moment? Or was it his wife who had succumbed in the dangerous moments of birth? His tears told me that whatever had just transpired had changed him, and his life, irrevocably.

So why do I think of this heartbroken stranger now, a decade later, during the sweltering summer when the heat shimmers off the white stones of my home, and my children suck sticky popsicles? Why has this picture moved from the inner recesses of my mind to a far more prominent position? Because *Tishah B'Av*, the day we mourn the destruction of the two Batei Mikdash and all that they meant, is approaching.

Midrash Eichah relates that there was a woman who lived in the neighborhood of Rabban Gamliel. She had lost her son, and every night she would weep profusely. Rabban Gamliel would hear her, and would himself shed bitter tears over the *churban*, the destruction of the Beis HaMikdash.

We may wonder how one set of tears connects with the other. R' Mordechai Gifter explains that every tragedy is rooted in the fact that the world has not yet reached its ultimate purpose. When our *galus* will end, so will all sorrow. Rabban Gamliel heard the woman sob over the death of her son, but he understood that the reason and root of her suffering was the *churban*. He then cried over the loss of the Beis HaMikdash.

This is a sobering thought.

We are barraged with stories of horrific grief: Of young widows left with tiny orphans. Of children battling for their lives. Of marriages unraveling and parents estranged from their offspring. All this heartbreak has one root, one source — the fact that we are still in *galus*.

Merely thinking of what we lost when the Beis HaMikdash disappeared in flames is difficult enough. There were ten miracles that took place on a daily basis in the Beis HaMikdash; ten ways Hashem would tell us "I am here, My child, right with you." In the times of the first Beis HaMikdash, we were surrounded by prophets. No gut-wrenching nights of lost sleep trying to come to "the right decision," no agonizing over paths not taken. One could discover what Hashem wanted, and the course of action that would lead to ultimate fulfillment, with ease. At the close of the *avodah* on Yom Kippur, the nation would look at the scarlet thread they had tied to the Beis HaMikdash door — if it had turned snow-white, they knew, with a certainty we cannot even fathom, that their sins had been forgiven.

The Beis HaMikdash was the pipeline that connected us directly to all blessings from Above. It gave us material benefit — rain, health, prosperity. But it gave us much more; it gave us a constant exposure to the glory and greatness of Hashem's presence. It was a tangible manifestation of our relationship with Him. It was a forceful roar of truth, so different from the whispers we strain to hear today.

And all that is reason enough to mourn.

But to compound that loss, there is the reality of every loss we have ever sustained, both individually and collectively, since the day we entered *galus*. Every blood libel and pogrom, the Inquisition and the Holocaust, the lost soldiers and wounded infants, all rooted in one source.

And the pain becomes unbearable.

But that is the source of our salvation. For only when it reaches that point, only when we realize how shattered and broken we actually are, can we take the steps necessary to start becoming whole once again. By mourning, we actually bring closer the day when the Beis HaMikdash will stand once again in Yerushalayim. The day the world will reach its ultimate purpose. The day when you, I, and the heartbroken stranger will enter a glorious period of endless revelation.

ELUL / אלול

Return

"Ani l'dodi v'dodi li, I am to my Beloved and my Beloved is to me, encapsulates the month of Elul. From the first day of the month," Hashem brings Himself toward His nation, becoming ever closer. Hashem is here. Do we avail ourselves of the opportunity? Do we grasp the awesome chance that is ours?

The challenge of Elul is the fact that the physical demands of our life continue unabated; if anything, they accelerate. There is laundry to clean and dishes to wash, deadlines to meet and meetings to attend; there is the Yom Tov meat-order and the new dresses the girls need. The King is at our doorstep, yet so often we scurry right by Him as we rush on with the mundane demands of our life. If we allow it, the voice of our body will drown out the cry of our soul.

Our children — our spiritual continuity — offer a host of opportunities which we can grasp twelve months a year. We have numerous chances to help them build their middos, enhance their emunah, and deepen their ahavas Yisrael. But how often do the opportunities come and go, slipping by as we hurry to feed, bathe, and bed down their bodies, forgetting to focus on their souls? Let this Elul, and the coming year, be the one in which we grow closer to our Creator, and bring our children along with us.

Crooked

My baby girl has a crooked head. My husband and I noticed it about a month ago. The crown of her head is not in the center of her skull, giving her an unbalanced look.

"She's such a thinker, her brain is having a meltdown," my brother quipped.

"You're the Lopsided Lady," we'd tease.

"You should take her to a doctor," my mother said.

And I knew she was right. But it was just before we left for vacation. And don't babies often have all sorts of strange bumps and protrusions that right themselves on their own? I promised myself I'd deal with the issue as soon as we got back. But then I was drowning in deadlines and laundry. I figured I'd wait until we had to visit the doctor for another matter, and ask then.

So a few weeks passed. I was in the park one Shabbos afternoon, schmoozing with half-a-dozen other melting mothers, when my baby's head came up in conversation. "Oh, don't worry too much. A lot of babies look funny, and then the skull corrects itself as it hardens," was the general consensus.

One mother disagreed. She had just come back from the States where a surgeon had operated on her baby's cleft palate. "This can be serious," she told me gravely. "The surgeon who treated my son works with everything connected to the head. He does surgeries on babies with crooked skulls. I'd see a doctor immediately." I gulped.

Two days later, we were at the doctor. He seemed to think it was rather serious as well. My baby has torticollis, he explained, a condition in which some of the muscles of the neck are tender, making it painful to turn in a particular direction. Often the condition begins with a crooked skull. And since the head is perpetually turned in just one direction, the soft bones of the newborn's skull continue to be pushed off-center. The doctor reassured me that the condition could be treated, but that it was essential that we start treatment immediately. We were to go regularly for physical therapy sessions. And, just to be safe, we should see a pediatric orthopedist. And perhaps a neurologist as well. More gulping.

I went home and started reading up on the condition. According to what I read, physical therapy is usually sufficient to treat torticollis. However, if left untreated, the condition can lead to a variety of long-term problems, including loss of motion of the neck, neurological problems, permanent facial asymmetry, and the need for cranial surgery.

I called the physical therapist immediately. "Torticollis," she said knowingly, "that's rather common. How old did you say she is? Four months? That's pretty old to start therapy for this condition." The waves of guilt threatened to engulf me.

"It will take a week or so to sort out the bureaucracy. Until then, make sure to give her lots of time on her stomach. And do everything you can to get her to look in the other direction. It's all a matter of practice. If she turns the other way over and over again, the muscles will become stronger."

So we started our campaign. I give her tummy time in the morning, my husband lies on the floor with her in the evening. We also keep her to the left of all activity, which forces her to turn her neck to the right. It was astonishing to see how after just a few short days, there was already slight improvement. She could turn to the right more easily and for longer periods of time.

This afternoon I took the baby to the pediatric orthopedist. He echoed what the other professionals had said. "Both the torticollis and the odd-shaped head are due to how she was positioned in utero. The head should straighten itself out by the time she's two years old. The neck needs exercise if you want it to be cured. Make sure to get her physical therapy. But this should all work out; don't worry."

I exhaled for the first time that week.

A few days ago, I had the *zechus* to speak with a premier educator in connection to an article I was writing. He mentioned the importance of constantly working to build relationships with our children. "It's always *mañana*, tomorrow, as the Spanish are fond of saying. Tomorrow we'll start the diet, speak with our children, devote time to our spouse. After all, our family is not going anywhere, so we can be better parents and spouses another day. But one day you wake up, and your kids are nearly adults. And you have nothing to do with them."

His words resonated. Yes, my baby's head didn't look great. But it wasn't awful either. I'll get to the doctor — tomorrow. I'll deal with it — soon. And in the meantime, the damage is insidiously taking place, until one day it's irreversible. *Baruch Hashem,*

I woke up in time to treat my daughter's neck and head. Hopefully she won't need surgery or suffer any long-term damage. But what about my children's souls? What about their thoughts and attitudes, which are being formed with every interaction we have?

The solution need not be daunting. At the moment, all my baby needs is tummy time, and a shift in where we place her. The physical therapist will give me some exercises for her neck. Success hinges not on monumental efforts, but on unwavering consistency. We need to work with her every single day. Five minutes here and ten minutes there, and suddenly she can swing her neck far more.

This works on the emotional level as well. Small, consistent positive interactions with a child will build a solid foundation that will be useful in later years. A hug, a compliment, a smile, a board game — do them often enough and great things will blossom.

Elul can be an overwhelming time of year. There is so much we want to change. We wish we were different. Yet change is in our grasp — if we can do it consistently. A *chessed* each day, an hour focused on proper speech, ten minutes of learning. And next year, we'll be able to turn our heads with so much more freedom; our line of vision taking in even greater heights.

Purity and Power

We say thank you to Ima,
As it's in her *zechus* we stand here;
It is from her we learn to daven
To Hashem Who is so near.

Twenty-seven first graders sang with all their hearts. Their hands waved in synchrony, their gold costumes glinted, their eyes glowed. I saw only one of them. My eyes were glued to my Menucha, my six-year-old about to get her first siddur.

The excitement had begun exactly thirty-eight days earlier, when the first-graders began their countdown to the great day. Before she would open her eyes in the morning, Menucha would mumble, "Just twenty-six more days," "Now there are only seventeen left."

Rehearsals took place twice each week, and they were serious, intense affairs. Again and again, the girls would practice the elaborate motions and memorize the beautiful lyrics. Determined to surprise me, Menucha would not sing anything at home, but she did regale me with endless details of who would stand where, how they would march on the stage, and what costumes they would wear. She invited Bubby and whispered the songs to Tatty. We offered to make refreshments and planned every detail of the big morning.

Suddenly, there was just one day left — and then party morning dawned. Menucha called Bubby three times to ensure she'd be on time. She had me comb her hair in her favorite style. She fluttered around me as I prepared the trays of vegetables and parsley dip. I was getting a knot in my stomach from the tension.

The knot unwound when we got to the small hall with time to spare, and she eagerly donned her yellow belt, tie and headband. The music started and the singing began. Menucha's brow furrowed as she concentrated on remembering the words and doing each motion correctly. Every few minutes, she'd dart a glance at Bubby and me out of the corner of her eye, and her face would light up. I'd beam back.

The first song spoke about *tefillah* in general. Then, three girls stepped forward, one dressed as a grandmother, one as a mother, and one as a girl. This song focused on *tefillah* as a chain connecting the generations. I squirmed in my seat. Is my *tefillah* as exemplary for my children as it should be? Next, there was an elaborate song-skit comparing davening to a pipe; just as one transports water, the other brings down berachah.

A short break was followed by a slide show. The girls appeared one-by-one on the screen, each bent over her siddur, and then a paper with their personal *tefillah* was shown. The girls' wishes were touching in their purity — "Help me be a good girl and listen to my parents," "Let Mashiach come soon." Some were poignant. "Help me not to hit," asked a girl who I knew had social difficulties. "Let nothing bad happen anymore," penned the child whose grandfather had passed away just several weeks earlier.

As the event neared its climax and the girls were about to receive their siddurim, they sang a song thanking their mothers, and speaking of how they hoped to daven just like us. I was distinctly uncomfortable at this point. I thought of the glow in Menucha's eyes each time she mentioned her siddur. I thought of her carefully articulating the words of *tefillah*. I thought of the excitement she had at the prospect of davening from a text.

No, little one, I wanted to say, let *me* daven like *you*. Let me have your innocence, your exuberance, your concentration. Let my *tefillah* be as pure as yours. I felt ashamed to think of my own Shacharis. A quick affair, said while I'm still blurry with sleep, far from the spiritual experience I wish it would be. What do I have to teach her?

But there are other *tefillos*. Not the formal ones said at morning and noon, but the ones I say all through the day. As I dial the doctor's office, I daven that I should get through this time and be able to ask about the baby's mysterious rash. There is the *tefillah* I whisper when I send off a story to a potential publisher. "Let us be blessed with plentiful *parnassah*." Some are said in a strangled tone, as the kids bicker, and I feel my pulse rising. "Help me deal with this properly; let me not say anything I will regret." When I see an email from my wonderful friend, still single and lonely, a prayer rises to my lips, asking that she find the right one soon.

I may not have innocence, but that very lack is what fuels so many of my requests. I know what can go wrong. I've seen disappointment, heartbreak, and pain. While I try not to dwell on any of these possibilities, the knowledge of their existence gives my prayers an intensity that my daughter's cannot possibly have.

She, of course, knows nothing of this, is unaware of my ongoing conversation with my Father and King throughout the course of the day. All she sees is my whispering Shacharis as she rushes out the door. I long for her innocence and purity. And I want to transmit to her the power and potential of the words she says.

Can you give what you yourself have not yet obtained? Can my yearning to tap more deeply into the words used for centuries somehow touch her? Can she be inspired by my aspiration, if my actions don't yet match up? And how does one transmit the message that *tefillah* is not just what you do, it's who you are? How do I convey to her that her siddur should be but the beginning of her talking to her Creator?

I have no answers, know of no formulas. So I do the only thing left to do — look upward and ask.

First-Day Knot

She laid out his clothes; first the new black pants, and then the freshly-ironed pinstriped shirt. Then Dina stood back for a moment to look at the outfit from a distance. Yes, it was just right; it would make the wearer look put-together and well cared-for without looking stuffy. At least, that was the impression she hoped the teacher would get. She added underwear and a new pair of socks to the pile, gave her sleeping son a kiss on the forehead, and tiptoed out. She'd best be going to sleep herself; tomorrow was a big day.

In bed, she had a hard time falling asleep. In just a few hours she'd be launching three of her children back into the world of school. They'd have new teachers, new schedules, new seats. So many things to worry about. Her thoughts drifted to each of her children. Shani, her responsible oldest, was a serious student. In fact, she often took school too seriously. Dina wished she could erase the tiny crease that was already appearing between Shani's eyes. The crease that deepened whenever a report was due or a final nearing. Dina wanted her to have a carefree childhood, to luxuriate in the blithe beauty of youth, but Shani couldn't seem to allow herself to let go — ever.

That wasn't Shalom's problem. Dina had the lines memorized by now. "Shalom clearly has much potential — he simply needs to apply himself." "If Shalom would devote just half his energies to school work, he would be at the top of the class." Sure, he was popular with every boy in the school and was friendly to all people — even the bus driver and custodian who were ignored by the others — but that wasn't the yardstick his teachers used to measure success.

Then there was Moishy, sweet, timid Moishy. It pained her every time she saw him step on that big yellow bus. Each day, he'd set out full of good will, hoping the others would like him and play with him. And each day, he'd step off the bus hours later with the bruised look of defeat stamped upon his delicate features. She still couldn't figure out what it was about him that seemed to bring out the cruelest streak in his classmates' nature. She'd tried sending him with nosh for the others, she made sure his clothing was exactly what the others were wearing, she coached him in social skills. Yet his wings continued to be crushed day after day, until she feared he'd never fly.

She had finally fallen into a fitful sleep when the baby roused her with his piercing screams. She stumbled to his room, and reached out for him. He settled down to eat, and she rubbed her nose against his downy head, inhaling the fragrance of baby. She gazed upon the tiny human being cradled in her arms. One day, he too would have to leave the cocoon of her love. How would those hours apart change him? In what way would school test his mettle? What prayers would she whisper as he walked out the door?

When the alarm rang at six-thirty, she blinked in surprise. Why had she wanted to wake up at such an early hour? Then, she remembered the significance of the day and hurried downstairs to fix a hot breakfast. Breakfast underway, she set about waking her brood. Shani was already dressed, checking the contents of her backpack yet again. Shlomo was still under the covers, refusing to budge; and Moishy was struggling with his socks, an inscrutable expression upon his face. She calmed Shani, shook Shlomo, and rebuttoned Moishy's shirt.

An hour later, the house was quiet, but Dina's insides churned. She resisted the urge for another cup of coffee, and decided to tackle the daunting pile of ironing she'd been neglecting during the lazy days of summer. There was something almost therapeutic about sliding the iron again and again over the fabric and watching the creases vanish, the bumpy surface transformed into a smooth, unbroken expanse.

After the ironing, she made the beds and straightened up the bedrooms, threw in a load of laundry, and washed the breakfast dishes. In between tasks, she fed and bathed the baby. With a start, she realized that this morning looked just like every other morning of her life. It was identical to the endless procession of mornings which stretched both behind and ahead of her, as far as her inner eye could see. It was only the knot in her stomach which was different.

That knot — what would it take to untie it? Would being granted a peek at each of her children at this very moment, as they navigated the rocky waters of scholastic demands and social pressure, allow her to relax? Or would it simply tie the knot tighter? Was it the future she needed to know — a brief glimpse at each of her children at the end of the tunnel called school, beyond the worries and problems that currently plagued them? But then there'd be new problems — larger problems — to take their place.

Her own life was so unchanging — a never-ending stream of duties and tasks. It was only through her children that she experienced the bittersweet intensity of endings and beginnings.

Dina glanced at her watch. It was past noon. Time to put together a meal, so that Moishy would have a hot lunch waiting for him when he arrived back from the battlefield. Glancing at her watch once more, she decided she'd have just enough time to bake a batch of cookies before making the calzones she'd planned for lunch. She took out the mixer, laid out her ingredients, and began to hum.

The Ex-Kvetch

We were the kvetch club, although we'd never dubbed ourselves as such. Chaya and I could always vent to each other: In the morning after our babies didn't allow us to get any work done; in the afternoon when we'd commiserate about toddlers' tantrums and siblings' altercations; and late, late at night when we'd scramble to get our work in before deadlines, while rocking colicky newborns.

We were both so busy that we rarely had the luxury of a long conversation. But email allowed us to give each other a blow-by-blow report of the hardships of our lives. "Baby just woke up for the third time tonight. Still have two hours of work ahead of me, and it's already one a.m!" "House looks like it was hit by a hurricane, and my cleaning help just quit. On top of that, two kids are sick ...." "Went for an ultrasound this morning and had to wait two full hours! It killed my whole morning." "In-laws are coming in three days. I haven't a thing in the freezer, and there's this massive project due in two days. Help!"

We didn't just complain — our friendship was woven from many threads. We chatted, we philosophized, we marveled, and we pondered. But Chaya was my favorite address when I craved a good kvetch, sparing my husband from needing to listen to at least some of my laments. No matter how bad things got — and some days were really rough — the knowledge that I could chronicle it all, send it across cyberspace to Chaya, and receive unconditional commiseration, made it just a tad easier to bear.

With our kids nearly the same age, and working at the same profession, we each perfectly understood the difficulties the other faced. In fact, sometimes our conversations sounded like we were vying for the position of "least rested" or "most overwhelmed". We were always on the same page.

This idyllic state of affairs changed very abruptly a few weeks ago. First the emails sounded different. I'd write, "Baby better be teething because she hasn't stopped crying all day." Instead of getting back, "Don't I know it. Miri's molars are coming in and it's a nightmare!" There'd be a sympathetic, "Hope your evening will be better than your day." And then Chaya would move on to some news flash in her life.

Then the phone calls changed their flavor. I'd tell her about the bureaucratic hassles I was dealing with while trying to get my baby physical therapy, and she'd listen politely and validate my frustration. But there was no "Isn't it tough?" No "In this country, your baby can start going on shidduchim before they sort the therapies out." No rebuttal kvetch.

It took me a few days to catch on, but it soon became apparent that I was the only one doing any complaining. Chaya was empathetic, but perpetually upbeat. I began to wonder what was going on in her home. Had her clingy baby suddenly become fully independent? Had her two sons ceased their bickering? Had her toddler's erratic sleep habits disappeared overnight?

"Sounds like things are really peachy over by you," I finally said. "I'm so happy for you."

"Actually, nothing in my life has changed," she replied, "except for my attitude."

What was that supposed to mean?

Chaya continued. "You know there's been so much bad news lately. Rochel's husband was diagnosed with cancer, other people I know are going through rough times, and it really got me thinking. *Baruch Hashem*, I'm so blessed. I have a husband, children, health, a home, a job. My problems are so trivial compared to the really big troubles life can send one's way. How can I complain?

"So the baby gets up at night. But now I'm so glad I have a baby. And that she's healthy. And that I'm healthy and can care for her. So my house is a mess. But that means that I have a home and toys to fill it and children to mess it. It's funny, there are still all the same challenges, but now I see them through different eyes. My life seems quite wonderful.

"I'm not perfect," she hastened to add. "Of course I lose it sometimes, and fall into negativity. But generally, I'm just so grateful for all I have, that complaining just doesn't fit into the picture."

Hmmm. I was impressed, that was for sure. And a tad jealous. Her attitude sounded so fantastic. But so unattainable. I was too deeply entrenched in my ways. "Life's hard enough," a little voice inside said. "Shouldn't I at least have the pleasure of kvetching about it?" So I told her I thought her mindset switch was fabulous and that I wished her lots of luck. And then I looked around for someone else with whom I could kvetch.

But that wasn't so easy to find. I have a number of close friends. But few knew me quite as well as Chaya, and there were none with whom I was in such close, hour-by-hour contact. And even I realized that dumping all my frustrations into my husband's ears would poison our home atmosphere.

So, despite myself, I had to drastically cut down on my complaining. I had to look for other things to mention in my steady stream of emails to Chaya — other topics to discuss in our phone conversations. I'd think of some complaint I wanted to share, and then catch myself, unwilling to feel foolish in face of her positive attitude.

And I started noticing something surprising. Life, while still not a bed of roses, certainly seemed rosier. All the kvetching had felt good at the moment, but it reinforced negative thought-patterns. "Poor me," was the underlying message. "Yes, poor you," would be the reply. And "poor me" would feel even worse. Once I had to move past all the complaining, there was actually a large amount of good in my life. Not that I was focusing on it — that was Chaya's department — but once I took off my dark glasses, it just stared me in the face.

As Tishrei is coming upon us, and every empty spot in the city is filled with freshly-cut wooden boards, long rolls of *s'chach*, and fragrant *esrogim*, I find myself thinking about Chaya. Succos is called *chag ha'asif*, as it always falls out in the autumn, when farmers have just harvested their crops and have the sweet satisfaction of full silos and well-stocked pantries. It's also called *zman simchaseinu*, the time of our joy.

I reflect on how Chaya seems so much more content and at peace with herself lately. And I wonder — are the two not connected? Is the feeling of being blessed with bounty — of having all of one's needs — not inextricably intertwined with one's happiness?

Hmmm. Looks like the kvetch club may be losing its last member.

Kingdoms

*M*ost of the time, she skimmed through life on a speedboat. That was one of those slick crafts that flew across the waves, looking as though it was flitting above the water and not within it. There was so much to do and so little time in which to do it, that if she wanted to stay afloat, she had to work relentlessly, never daring to pause. She'd rush from work to home, from kitchen to laundry room, from child to child, until she'd collapse into bed so she could start the same thing the next day.

She did her jobs well. She was invaluable in the office — the only one who could handle ornery clients and the temperamental photocopy machine. She kept the cleanest house on the block. There was not a cobweb in her kingdom — even in the depths of her basement — and not one pair-less sock in the house. She was a proficient cook — people walked a mile to come to the *kiddushim* where her cherry-chocolate torte was to appear. Her children went to school every day on time and spotless, with their homework neatly completed and a nutritious lunch tucked into their knapsacks.

She reveled in her competence. It was the rock upon which her life was built; a solid constant in a frenzied world. And never did her competence exhibit even the slightest of cracks. Store-bought challah never entered her home. She had never missed a PTA meeting in the nearly two decades her children had been attending school. Her entire family was decked out in breathtaking, hand-sewn outfits every Yom Tov.

She felt the price she had to pay for such competence was fairly rewarded. Hard as it was to prepare apple strudel just days after birth, the sense of accomplishment she felt as she watched her guests savor every bite made it all worthwhile. Tricky as it was to show up early for a school play so she could help out behind stage, her daughter's glowing face and the teacher's gratitude kept her going.

The fall happened in Elul.

She believed that one should greet every Yom Tov, not just Pesach, with an immaculate home. She was climbing up a ladder to take down her drapes for washing when she lost her balance. One moment she was reaching for the tawny brocade, and the next, she was lying on the floor, her leg twisted in a gruesome position, and the pain so sharp that she felt she'd fly through the roof.

In the emergency room, she was informed that she had multiple breaks in her leg. It would need to be in a traction splint for at least two weeks. Luckily, she wouldn't need to be hospitalized. A nurse would come to her home and help her family set up the equipment she'd need.

So that's how she found herself three weeks before Rosh Hashanah, not making her famous pomegranate chicken or crafting elaborate cards, but lying flat on her back, helpless, and for the first time ever, incompetent.

She kept her laptop right beside her and sent dozens of emails to work each day, trying to manage the hectic office from afar. She typed up menus and shopping lists, and gave her teenagers a never-ending list of directives. But they were hindered by school work and a cavalier attitude.

Her husband finally convinced her to have the Yom Tov catered, although the thought of a store-bought honey cake turned her stomach. There was no way they added freshly-squeezed lemon juice and grated apple to their cakes as she would have done! She pretreated the laundry that was brought to her bedside, and implored her family to clean up all stovetop spills immediately. But no one cared the way she did. Her perfectly run kingdom was dissolving like a sand castle caught in the tide.

When there was nothing else she could do from her supine position, she'd stare out the huge picture window next to her bed. She had never really taken in the view from her window, never lain in bed long enough to notice it. Now, though, she drank in the details — the huge trees ablaze with the colors of fall, the last of the birds flying by on their journey to warmer lands, the spunky squirrels which scampered past, clutching nuts in their paws.

When the view outside lost its luster, she was forced to train her gaze inward. And she realized with a start that, much as she had been oblivious to the view outside her window, she was equally unfamiliar with the terrain of her heart. Her life had been so focused on the where, when, and how, that she had never asked — Why?

Why have a pristine home? Why make homemade gefilte fish? Why send children to school with avocado dip and freshly-cut vegetables neatly tucked into shiny lunchboxes? Why?

It was amazing how all her self-evident truths, all the axioms upon which she had predicated her life, seemed to dissolve once they were placed under the scrutiny of that burning question. Had it all been purposeless? She knew that wasn't the case either. So what was the purpose?

A friend, hearing of her fall, brought her the latest frum novels — books she normally would never have the time to read, and dropped off a few Torah tapes as well. One morning, when the quiet of the large house seemed to scream, she slipped one of the tapes into the mini-stereo by her bed.

The speaker was discussing the Rosh Hashanah davening, focusing on the Mussaf prayer. Unlike many of the other speakers she had heard over the years at the shiurim she had attended during Elul, he didn't discuss individual words or phrases. Instead, he asked his audience to think of the concepts.

"'Say before Me the *pesukim* of *malchuyos*, so that you should accept My kingship upon you,' we are told. But what is the essence of kingship?" the speaker asked. "How can we coronate our King?"

She paused the tape for a moment and allowed her mind to wander. She knew all about kingdoms; she had ruled one until recently. But there was the rub, was it not? Who was meant to be the ruler of her kingdom? She turned the tape back on.

"We must choose to live our life with Hashem at its core. He should be the reason we go through our day; the focus of each move we make. He's the reason we live and the reason we die. We make Him King when our actions, our thoughts, our dreams revolve around Him and His will. On Rosh Hashanah, our job is to realign ourselves with this vision."

And in a flash, she realized she had just received the key to answering all her whys.

Uncork the Love

*D*earest Akiva,

Today was your eighth birthday. You received a card and cash from Bubby and Zaidy, and a promise of a gift from us. We had chocolate pudding for breakfast, your favorite spread in the lunch sandwiches, and you were able to pick anything you wanted for supper. You chose pizza, and beamed with pride as you distributed it to your siblings. Then, when Tatty came home especially early, we went out together — just you and me.

First we went to buy you sandals. Although we all went shoe shopping just last week, you didn't find the exact style that you liked. So now we went to a more expensive store, where we found the style *you* liked, in the color I wanted. I tried to ignore the price tag, and we both left happy.

We did a few small errands — bought some whole-wheat flour at the health-food store, picked up stockings for the girls at a sock shop, and took money out of an ATM machine. When I go with you, every purchase becomes an adventure. Your perpetual curiosity picks up on the details I would never notice — the unusual bike helmet someone is wearing, the gallon-jug of molasses at the health-food store, the brick oven in the pizza parlor we passed. You have an endless thirst for experiences — to try to work the cash register, to figure out how money emerges from a machine, to try a new health bar at the health-food store. Often that thirst leaves me feeling depleted. Today, I just looked on lovingly, answered the stream of questions, and made sure nothing was harmed.

We went to the book store where you picked out a birthday present. I enjoyed watching you fondle the books, peek into so many of them, and deliberate over which one to choose. I myself was doing the same, and I could fully appreciate your feelings.

Our last stop was the park. We had stopped at the bakery earlier, and you had picked out two luxuriant triple-chocolate ice-cream bars. Now we would enjoy them together. We selected a bench that faced away from the street, and sat down close to each other. You leaned against my shoulder. We pulled off the shiny wrappers and started licking our treats.

We didn't say much, you and I, even though we are both big talkers. We watched the stragglers still on the swings, soaring into the darkening sky, the teens roaming the area, and the men hurrying by as they cut through the park to reach their homes after a long day. I sucked the chocolate coating until it melted, sliver by sweet sliver, sliding down my throat. You took big chunks out of your bar, the chocolate adorning your face, hands, and shirt.

Earlier that day, I had turned to Tatty while he looked over my shoulder, reading an article I had just completed.

"It's 2:30," I said wistfully. "Eight years ago, Akiva was just ten minutes old. Remember how we felt?"

A touch of the incandescent joy which had been ours on that long-ago day infused Tatty's face as he murmured, "Yes, we were so happy." We sat for a moment letting that exultation — the indescribable happiness of having become parents — pass over us once more.

Then Tatty gestured to the screen and said, "You left out the word 'is' in that sentence."

Now, as we ate our ice cream, and the stars began to gleam in an ebony sky, and the crickets to chirp their song in the bushes around us, I searched for a way to pass on to you the feelings I had had for you at that moment.

"Tatty and I were remembering the day you were born," I told you. "We were so happy when you joined our family. We are so glad you're our boy."

You beamed at me.

I looked at you. You seemed so big — broad shoulders, a solid build, a full head taller than every other kid in your class. Your pants were spattered with dirt, and your shirt grubby from a long day of being a boy. It was so hard to juxtapose this reality with my mental snapshot of the tiny infant I had been handed eight years before. That boy had been delicate as a flower petal, fragile as a baby bird. He had smelled so sweet, and I loved nuzzling my nose into his cheek. He had been helpless and utterly dependent. And the love — it had been so deep — I ached from the intensity.

Looking at you, and thinking of that baby, I felt a rush of deep sadness. The love then had been so pure, so complete. It was the same love I was feeling now; joy and pride and tenderness all mixed together. There had been no anger, no battle of wills, no disobedience, no impatience, no defiance. What happened to us? How have I allowed the beauty of our relationship to slip out of my consciousness so often, drowned out by your acting as little boys will? Why do I allow the frustrations and tensions of raising a strong-willed, determined, and active son obscure the tender feelings I harbor within?

If only I could have bottled the feelings I had then, as the midwife handed me a tiny, perfect human being. If only I could trap the ones I have now, as you sit next to me, bristling with energy, yet sipping in the togetherness we are sharing. I would open the bottle and take a whiff each time I find myself losing sight of your preciousness.

We lick the last remnants of our treat. Slowly, we gather our bags, throw away our sticks, and walk home together.

I love you so much, my big one,

Mommy